SCOTTISH CERTIFICATE OF EDU

Credit and General
CRAFT & DESIGN

The Scottish Certificate of Education Examination Papers
are reprinted by special permission of
THE SCOTTISH QUALIFICATIONS AUTHORITY

ISBN 0 7169 9295 7

ROBERT GIBSON · Publisher
17 Fitzroy Place, Glasgow, G3 7SF.

SCOTTISH CERTIFICATE OF EDUCATION

CRAFT AND DESIGN
STANDARD GRADE

Time — GENERAL LEVEL — 1 hour

Time — CREDIT LEVEL — 1 hour

INSTRUCTIONS TO CANDIDATES

1 Answer all the questions.

2 Read every question carefully before you answer.

3 Write your answers in the spaces provided.

4 Do **not** write in the margins.

5 All dimensions are given in millimetres.

6 Before leaving the examination room you must give this book to the invigilator. If you do not, you may lose all the marks for this paper.

CONTENTS

SCOTTISH CERTIFICATE OF EDUCATION 1995

THURSDAY, 25 MAY
10.20 AM – 11.20 AM

CRAFT AND DESIGN STANDARD GRADE

General Level

ATTEMPT ALL QUESTIONS

1. A high street fashion store requires several shelving/display units for sweatshirts, T shirts, jeans, etc. A proposed design for the unit is shown below.

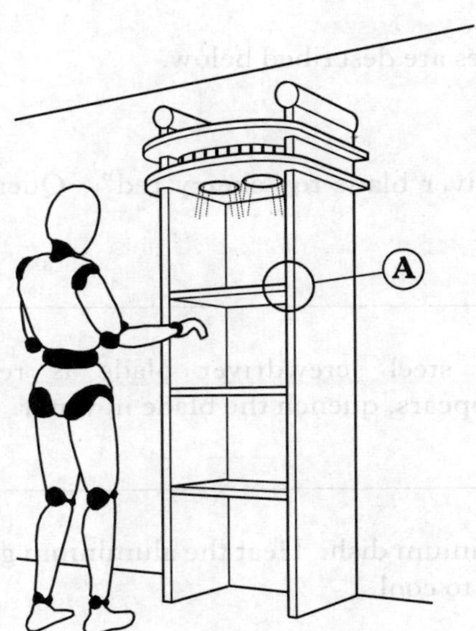

(*a*) (i) Suggest **two** different materials that would be suitable for making the sides of the units.

Material 1 ____________________ 1 0

Material 2 ____________________ 1 0

(ii) Select **one** of the materials chosen above and name one suitable finish that could be applied to this material.

Material chosen ________________ Finish ________________ 1 0

(*b*) List **three** methods of jointing the shelf to the unit at Ⓐ.

1. ____ 1 0

2. ____ 1 0

3. ____ 1 0

(*c*) Write down **two** pieces of information that would have to be found out before deciding on the dimensions for the units.

1. ______________________________________ 1

______________________________________ 0

2. ______________________________________ 1

______________________________________ 0

2. Three heat treatment processes are described below.

(*a*) Name each process.

1. Heat a steel screwdriver blade to "cherry red". Quench vertically in oil, brine or tepid water.

Process 1. ______________________________ 1 0

2. After cleaning, the steel screwdriver blade is reheated. When the appropriate colour appears, quench the blade in water.

Process 2. ______________________________ 1 0

3. Rub soap on an aluminium dish. Heat the aluminium gently until the soap turns black and leave to cool.

Process 3. ______________________________ 1 0

(*b*) What does process 3 do to the aluminium?

______________________________________ 1

______________________________________ 0

3. A proposed design for a candle holder is shown below.

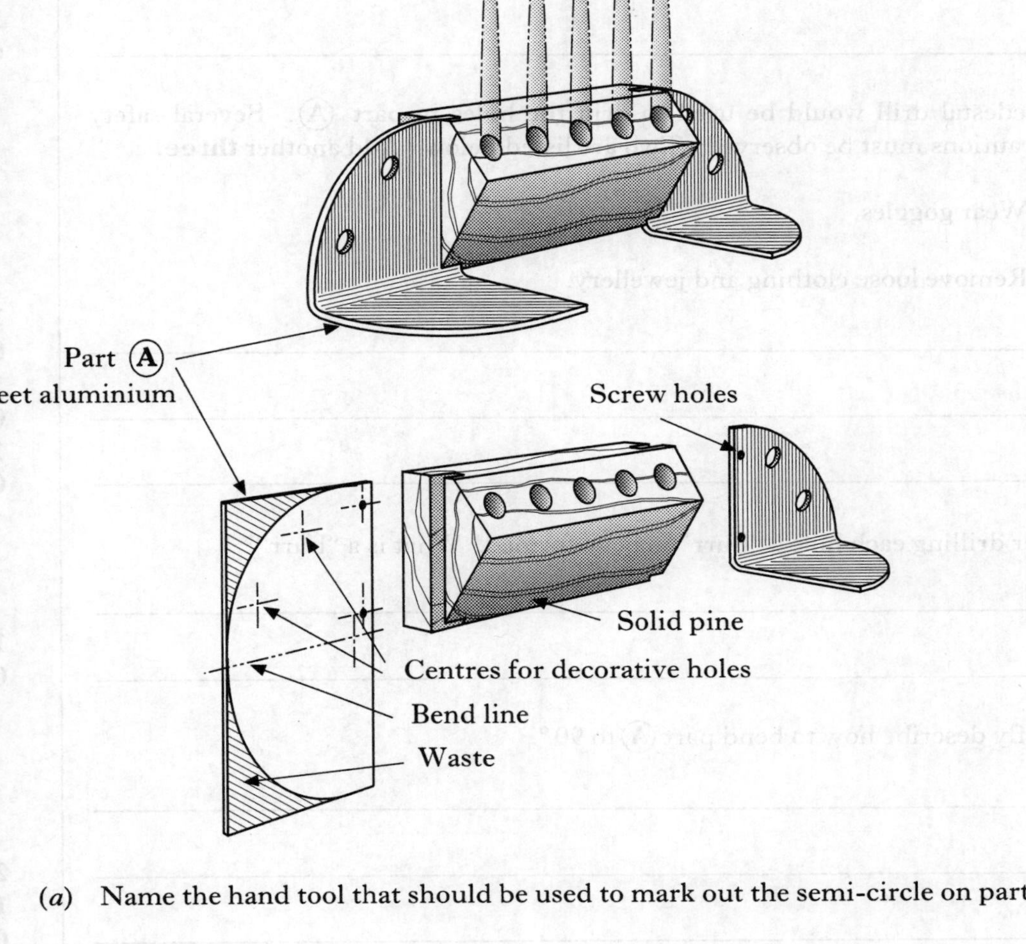

(*a*) Name the hand tool that should be used to mark out the semi-circle on part (A). **1 0**

____

(*b*) Which hand tool should be used to remove most of the waste material from part (A)? **1 0**

____

(*c*) Briefly describe how to smooth and finish the edges of part (A) to make it safe to handle. **3 2 1 0**

____

____

____

____

(*d*) Why should part Ⓐ be centre punched before drilling the holes?

____

____ 1 0

(*e*) A pedestal drill would be used to drill the holes in part Ⓐ. Several safety precautions must be observed. Two are listed below. Add another **three**.

1. Wear goggles.

2. Remove loose clothing and jewellery.

3. ____ 1 0

4. ____ 1 0

5. ____ 1 0

(*f*) After drilling each hole a "burr" may be formed. What is a "burr"?

____

____ 1 0

(*g*) Briefly describe how to bend part Ⓐ to 90 °.

____

____

____ 2 1 0

4. A design for a single bed for a child's bedroom is shown below, with part of the bed end shown in detail.

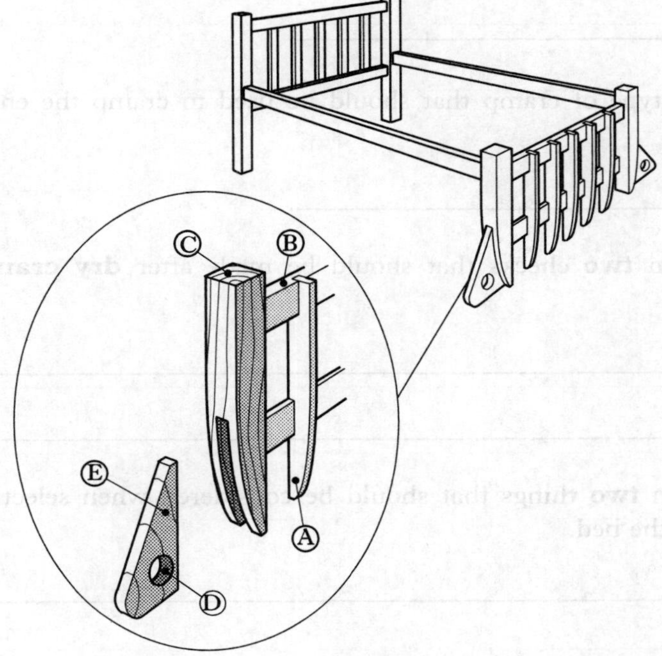

(*a*) What machine should be used to cut the curve at Ⓐ?

____ **1 0**

(*b*) Name a suitable joint that could be used to join parts Ⓑ to Ⓒ.

____ **1 0**

(*c*) (i) Which hand tool could be used to bore the hole at Ⓓ ?

____ **1 0**

(ii) How would you prevent the back of the wood from splitting when boring the hole?

____

____ **1 0**

(*d*) Part Ⓔ is to be made from solid timber. Write down **three** checks that should be made to the surfaces of part Ⓔ to ensure that they have been suitably prepared for the application of a finish.

1. ____ **1 0**

2. ____ **1 0**

3. ____ **1 0**

(*e*) Name a suitable finish for part Ⓔ.

_______________________________ 1 0

(*f*) Name the type of cramp that should be used to cramp the end frame of the bed.

_______________________________ 1 0

(*g*) Write down **two** checks that should be made after **dry cramping** the end frames.

1. _______________________________ 1 0

2. _______________________________ 1 0

(*h*) Write down **two** things that should be considered when selecting a **suitable** timber for the bed.

1. _______________________________ 1 0

2. _______________________________ 1 0

5. The items shown below can be used in lathe work. Name each item and briefly describe its use.

1
0

(*a*) Name ______________________________

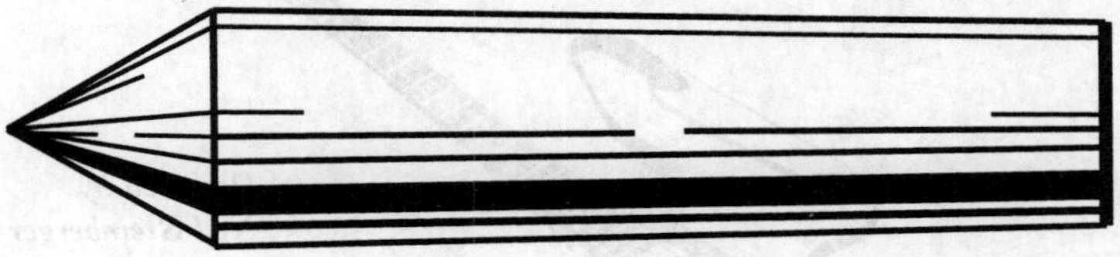

Use ______________________________

____

____

____

1
0

1
0

(*b*) Name ______________________________

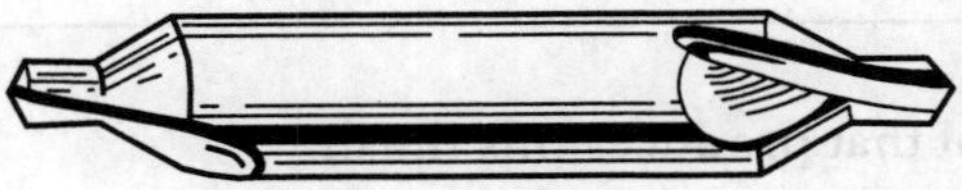

Use ______________________________

____

____

____

1
0

6. Some drawings of a design for a bass guitar are shown below.

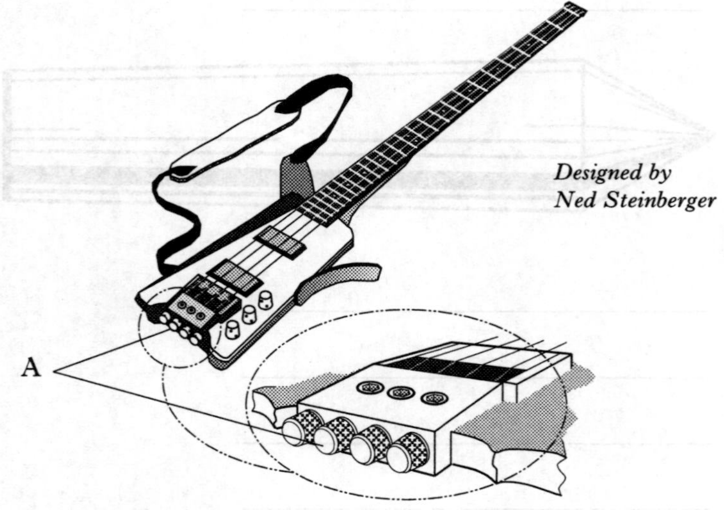

(*a*) Part A (tuning screw) should meet the following specification.

It must be hard wearing.

It must not rust.

It must look attractive.

Suggest a suitable material that could be used. ____________________ 1 0

(*b*) The tuning screws have a textured finish. Name the process carried out on the lathe to produce this finish.

____ 1 0

(*c*) Sketch the lathe tool that produces this finish.

1 0

(*d*) Before using a metalwork lathe several checks have to be made. Briefly describe **two** of these checks.

1. ____

____ 1 0

2. ____

____ 1 0

7. Ergonomics is an important part of telephone design.

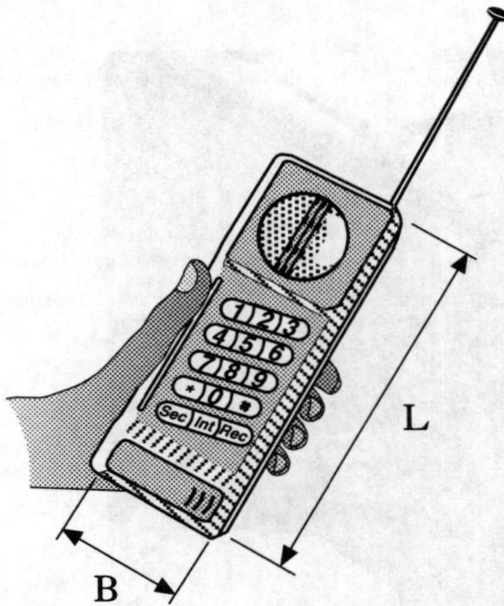

(*a*) For each of the following, what human factors should be considered when designing a telephone?

1. The size of the "dialling" buttons

____

______________________________ 1 0

2. The length L of the handset

____

______________________________ 1 0

3. The breadth B of the handset

____

______________________________ 1 0

(*b*) Suggest **one** way a design for a new telephone could be checked for comfort and ease of use before being mass produced.

____

______________________________ 1 0

(*c*) A suitable material needs to be chosen to make the casing for the telephone. Write down **two** properties that you would expect this material to have.

Property 1 ______________________________ 1 0

Property 2 ______________________________ 1 0

8. A designer has produced a new design for the interior of a railway carriage.

Suggest **three** things that are likely to have been in the specification given to the designer.

1. ____

____ 1 0

2. ____

____ 1 0

3. ____

____ 1 0

9. A pupil's design for a novelty clock made from acrylic sheet is shown below.

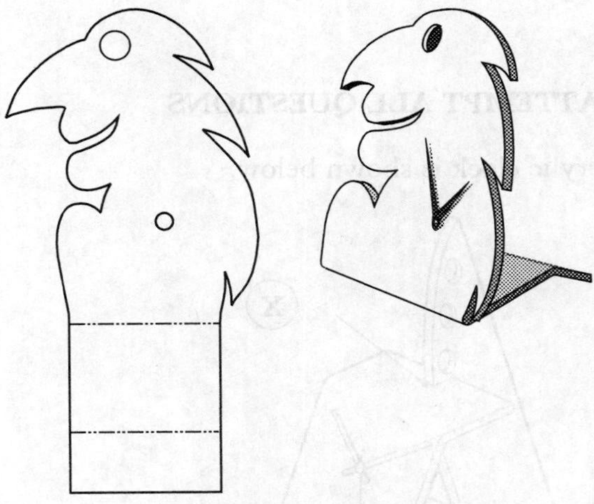

(*a*) Write down the main stages in the sequence of operations for making the clock.

____

____

____

____

____

____ 3 2 1 0

(*b*) The finished clock is to be evaluated. Add **two** further questions to the list below which could be used to evaluate the design.

(i) Does it look good?

(ii) Can the time be read easily?

(iii) ____ 1 0

(iv) ____ 1 0

[*END OF QUESTION PAPER*]

SCOTTISH CERTIFICATE OF EDUCATION 1996

MONDAY, 27 MAY
10.50 AM – 11.50 AM

CRAFT AND DESIGN STANDARD GRADE

General Level

ATTEMPT ALL QUESTIONS

1. A pupil's design for an acrylic clock is shown below.

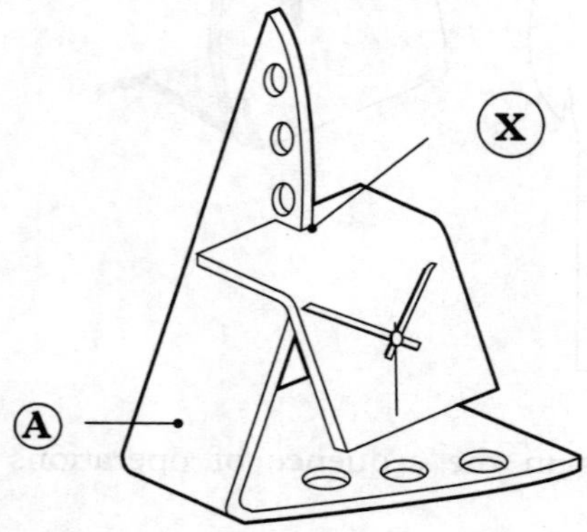

(*a*) There are two main types of plastics. Which type of plastic is acrylic?

______________________________ 1 0

(*b*) Name **one** hand tool that could be used to **cut** the curves on part Ⓐ.

______________________________ 1 0

(*c*) The holes on part Ⓐ have been drilled using a pillar drill.

(i) Apart from **goggles** and **clothing**, give **four** safety checks that should be taken **before** switching on the drill.

____

____

____

______________________________ 4

______________________________ 3 2 1

______________________________ 0

(ii) Name the tool used to hold part Ⓐ when drilling.

______________________________ 1 0

(*d*) Name the piece of equipment used to heat part (A) before bending.

1
0

(*e*) Suggest a method of joining the acrylic at (X). You may wish to use sketches to explain your answer.

1
0

(*f*) What is the functional advantage of the clock having a wide base?

1
0

2. A drawing of a drinks bar in a bowling alley is shown. The underside of the bar is used to store bowling balls.

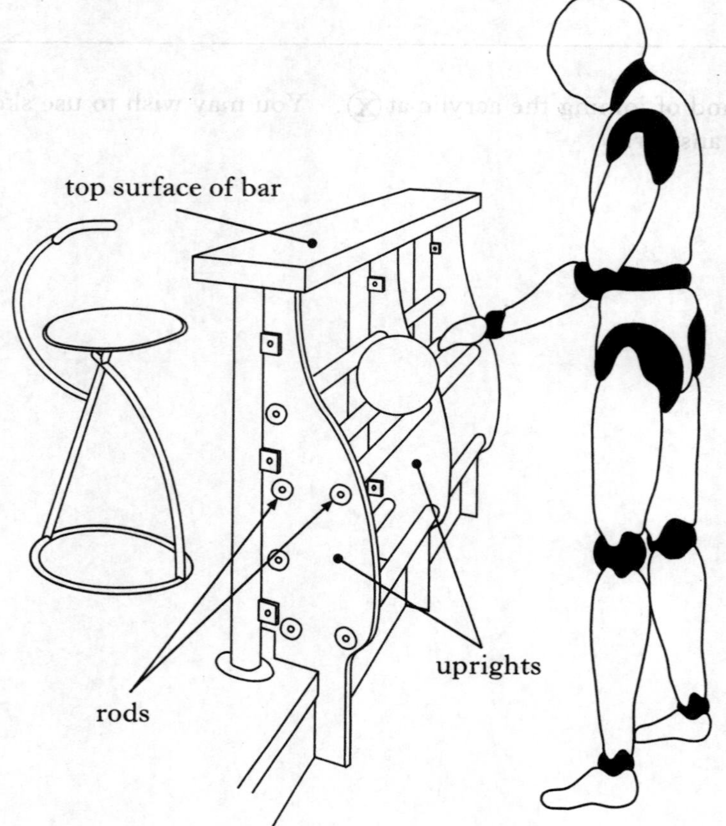

(*a*) The top surface of the bar is made from plastic laminate which cleans easily. Give **two** more properties of plastic laminate that make it a suitable material.

1. ***Cleans easily***

2. ________________________________

3. ________________________________

1
0
1
0

(*b*) Name **one** suitable man-made board that could be used for the uprights.

____

1
0

(*c*) For each of the following sizes, write down **one** piece of information that would have to be found out before or during the designing stage.

(i) The height of the top surface of the drinks bar

____ **1 0**

(ii) The distance between the uprights

____ **1 0**

(iii) The distance between the rods

____ **1 0**

3. A design for a wooden toy is shown below.

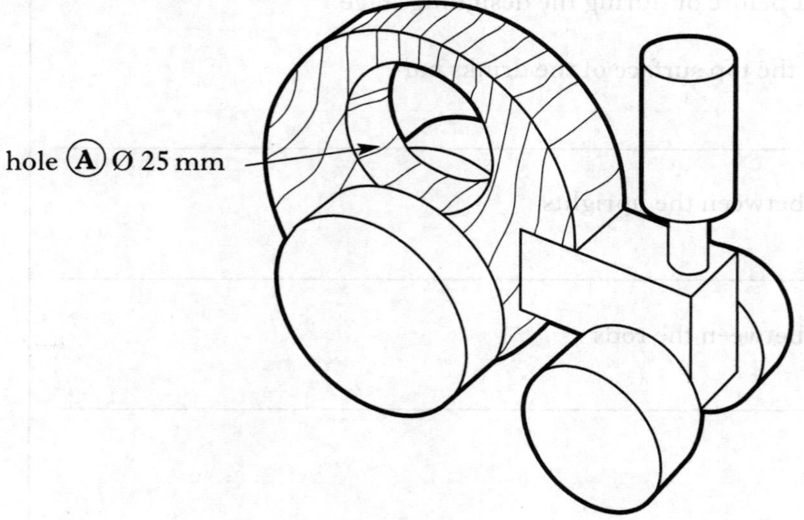

(*a*) The two large wheels are to be made on a lathe, from the block of wood shown below.

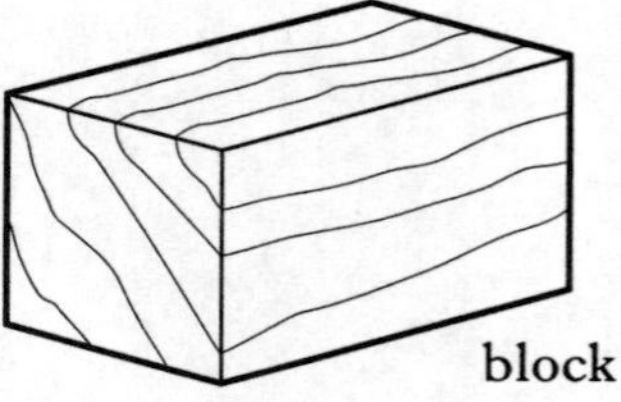

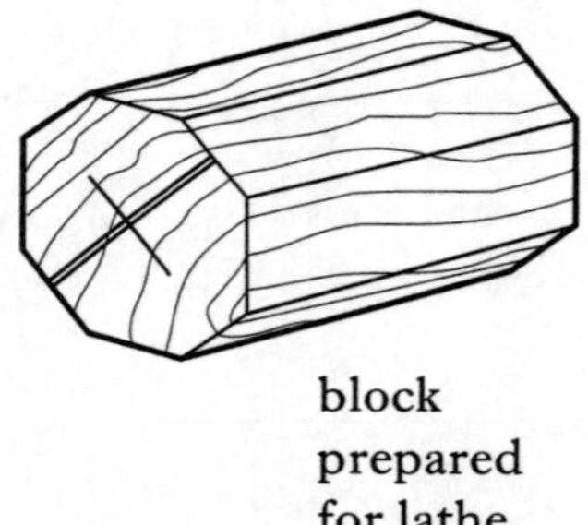

(i) Explain what could happen if the corners of the block were not removed before turning.

____ 1 0

(ii) Name the hand tool used to remove these corners.

____ 1 0

(iii) The wheels are shaped on a lathe. **Briefly describe how to**

turn the block

______________________________ 1 0

measure the turned block to see if it is the correct diameter for the wheels

______________________________ 1 0

get the two wheels to the correct thickness

______________________________ 1 0

separate one wheel and get it ready for drilling a hole for an axle.

______________________________ 1 0

(*b*) (i) Name the tool, used in a pillar drill, to cut the large hole (A).

______________________________ 1 0

(ii) What might happen to the wood if you did not drill the hole (A) through onto a flat wooden surface?

____

______________________________ 1 0

(*c*) List **three** requirements of a suitable finish for this toy.

1. ______________________________ 1 0

2. ______________________________ 1 0

3. ______________________________ 1 0

4. The chair shown below is made from solid timber.

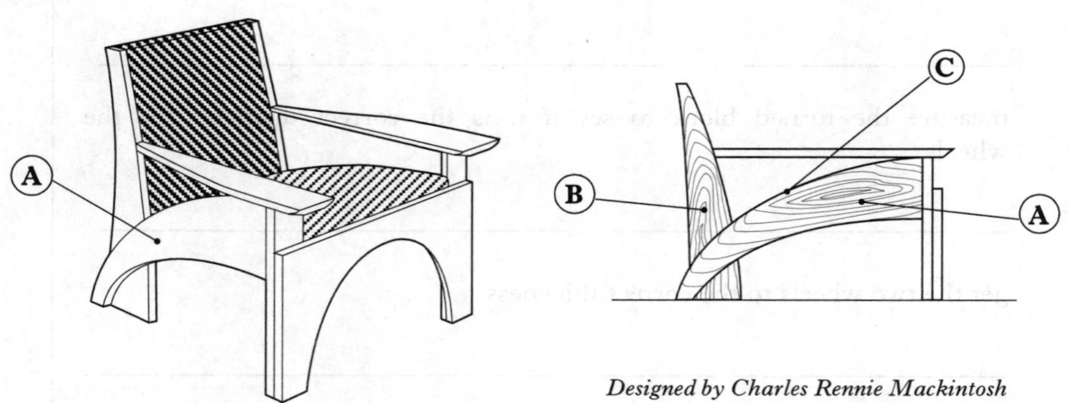

Designed by Charles Rennie Mackintosh

(*a*) Why was part (A) cut in a way that allows the grain to run along the length of the wood?

____

____ **1 0**

(*b*) Which machine should be used to cut the curves on part (A)?

____ **1 0**

(*c*) Describe how the curved edge (C) can be given a smooth finish using hand tools only. (You should name the hand tools used.)

____

____

____

____ **2 1 0**

(*d*) Suggest **one** wood joint that could be used to join part (A) to part (B).

____ **1 0**

(*e*) The chair is to be finished with a black stain. What would be the result of applying the stain to an area where

(i) glue had not been properly cleaned off

1 0

(ii) greasy fingerprints remained on the wood

1 0

(iii) faint pencil lines still remained on the wood?

1 0

5. The planning process for a pupil's design of a baby's high chair is outlined below. The titles of some of the main stages in this process are given.

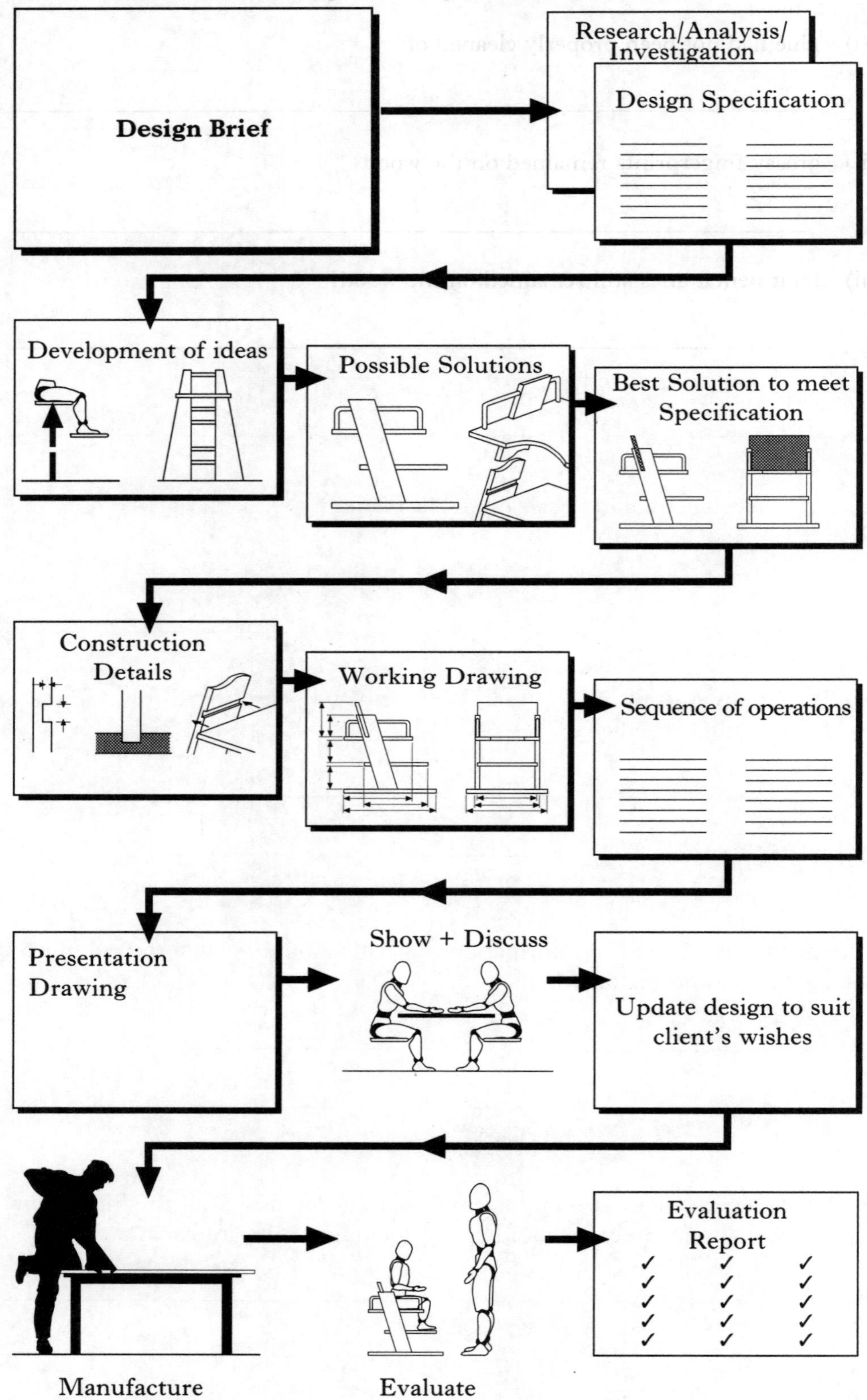

(*a*) Write down **three** things that should be included in the "design specification" for the high chair.

1. ______________________________ 1 0

2. ______________________________ 1 0

3. ______________________________ 1 0

(*b*) (i) What would be the main advantage of making a small scale model of the chair?

____

______________________________ 1 0

(ii) At what stage should a scale model be made?

____

______________________________ 1 0

(iii) Write down **two** things that could **only** be evaluated by testing a fully manufactured chair.

1. ______________________________ 1 0

2. ______________________________ 1 0

(*c*) Write down **two** pieces of information that you should be able to find out by looking at the "working drawing".

1. ______________________________ 1 0

2. ______________________________ 1 0

(*d*) Anthropometrics (sizes) are important factors in the design of the high chair. At what stage in the process should you be looking for this information?

______________________________ 1 0

6. A design for a wall clock is shown below. The dial is domed and has been cast in aluminium. The numbers are carried round on a chain which is driven by a small gear wheel.

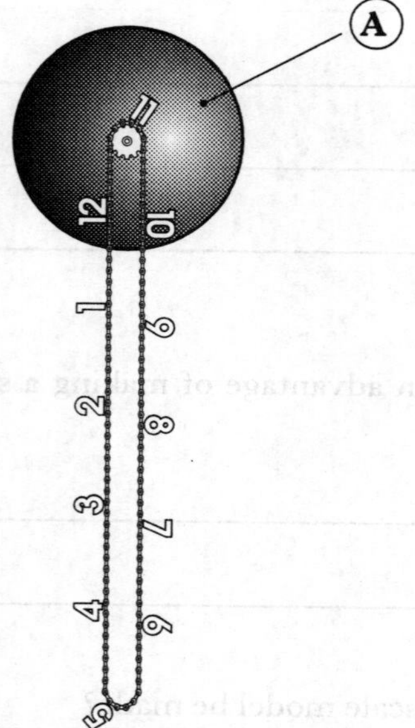

(*a*) A cross section of the casting boxes to be used when casting the dial Ⓐ is shown.

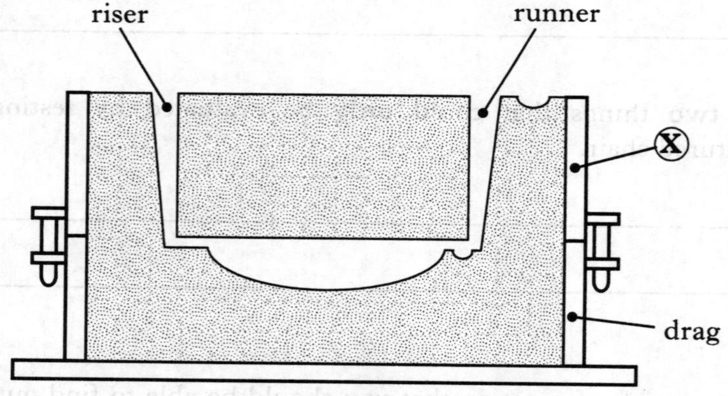

(i) What is the purpose of the runner?

1 0

(ii) What is the purpose of the riser?

1 0

(iii) Name part Ⓧ.

1 0

(*b*) What is the name given to the container in which the aluminium is melted?

____ **1 0**

(*c*) Give **one** reason why aluminium is regarded as a suitable metal for casting in a school workshop.

____

____ **1 0**

(*d*) (i) State **one** safety precaution to prevent molten aluminium, which may have overflowed or leaked out, from flowing across the floor and burning your feet.

____

____ **1 0**

(ii) Why should tongs be used when removing the casting from the moulding sand?

____

____ **1 0**

(*e*) The diagram below shows the casting after it has been removed from the boxes.

Describe how the excess metal would be removed.

____

____

____ **1 0**

7. A drawing of a design for a menu holder is shown below. The frame is made from solid wood and the centre is two pieces of glass.

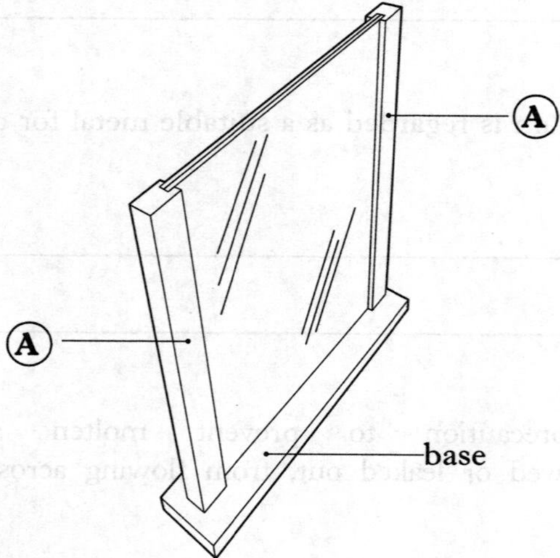

(*a*) (i) Write down **two** methods of joining parts (A) to the base.

1. ________________________ 1 0

2. ________________________ 1 0

(ii) Choose **one** of the above and write a sequence of operations describing how this would be **marked out**. (Your description should name all the tools used.)

____

____

____

____

________________________ 3 2 1 0

(*b*) When evaluating the finished holder, the designer found that the holder was easily knocked over and the glass broken.

(i) Suggest a lighter and safer material to replace the glass.

________________________ 1 0

(ii) Suggest a change to the base that would make the holder less likely to topple over.

________________________ 1 0

SCOTTISH CERTIFICATE OF EDUCATION 1997

MONDAY, 26 MAY
10.50 AM – 11.50 AM

CRAFT AND DESIGN
STANDARD GRADE
General Level

1 Answer all the questions.

2 Read every question carefully before you answer.

3 Write your answers in the spaces provided.

4 Do **not** write in the margins.

5 All dimensions are given in millimetres.

6 Before leaving the examination room you must give this book to the invigilator. If you do not, you may lose all the marks for this paper.

ATTEMPT ALL QUESTIONS

1. Shown below is a wall cabinet which will hold eight mugs.

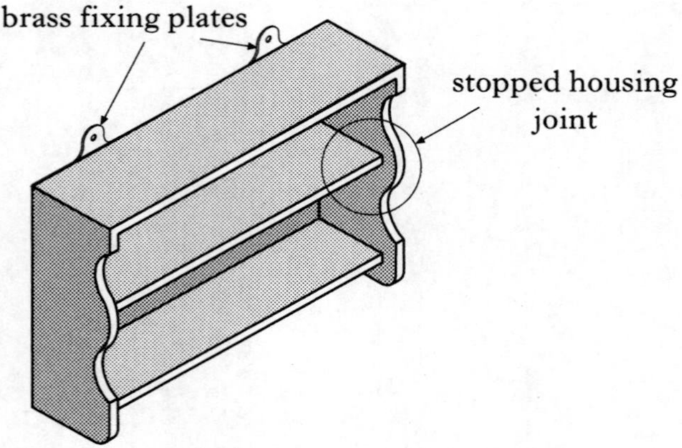

(*a*) (i) The number of mugs to be held in the cabinet was found at the investigation stage.
Write down **one** other piece of information about the mugs which will help in deciding the size of the cabinet.

____

____ **1 0**

(ii) Which dimension on the wall cabinet will this enable you to find?

____ **1 0**

(*b*) (i) Which hand tool would be used when marking lines across the face of the timber with a pencil?

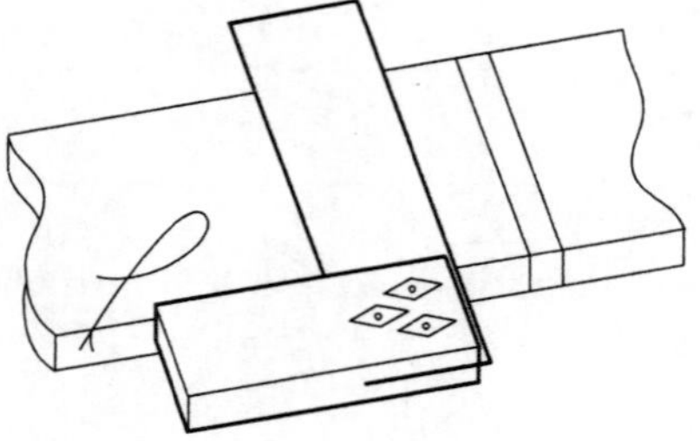

________________________ **1 0**

(ii) If the thickness of the timber was 12 mm, how deep should the stopped housing be?

______________ mm **1 0**

(iii) Name the hand tool that will mark a parallel line for the depth of the housing.

____ **1 0**

(*c*) Before assembly, all the inside surfaces should be cleaned to remove any marks. Give a reason for this.

____

____ **1 0**

(*d*) What type of cramp is shown below?

______________________________ **1 0**

(*e*) Explain the term "dry cramping".

____

____

____ **1 0**

(*f*) The cabinet is checked for squareness just after it has been glued and cramped. Describe **two** methods of checking for squareness.

Method 1 ____

____ **1 0**

Method 2 ____

____ **1 0**

(*g*) Name a suitable man-made board for the thin back of the cabinet.

____ **1 0**

(*h*) Two brass plates are used to fix the cabinet to the kitchen wall.

(i) Give a functional reason why **two** plates were chosen and not one.

____ **1 0**

(ii) Give a reason why brass was chosen for this purpose.

____ **1 0**

2. A student's design for a pencil holder is shown below.

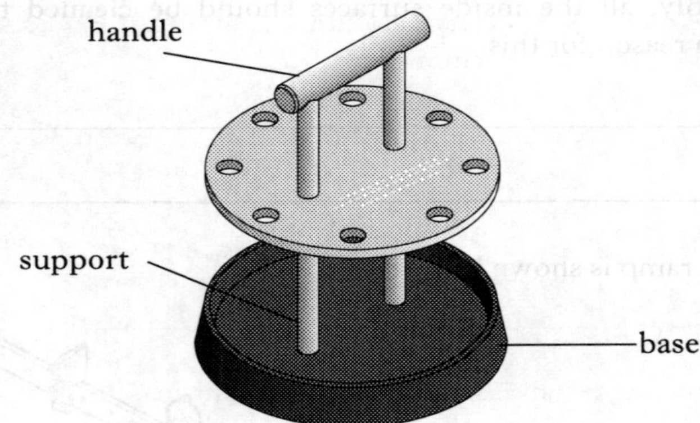

(*a*) During the research stage, the student had to investigate the various dimensions of pens and pencils.
Give a reason why the diameter of the pens and pencils is important.

____

____ 1 0

(*b*) The aluminium base will be cast and drilled in the school workshop.

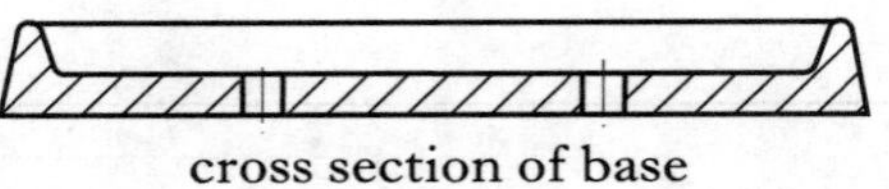
cross section of base

A sequence of operation for this process included some of the following terms and names.

(i) "Two boxes are used to hold the sand."

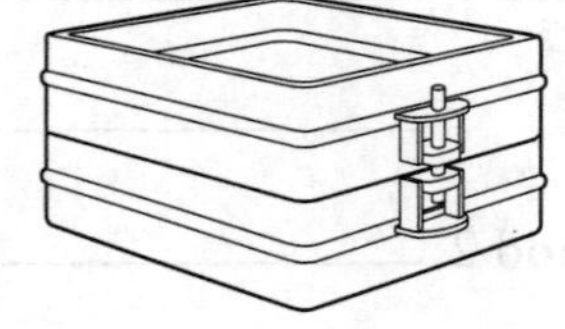

Name the **two** boxes. ______________ ______________ 2 1 0

(ii) "The pattern for the base needs a taper."

Explain the need for this taper. ______________________________

____ 1 0

(iii) "Dust the pattern with parting powder."

Explain the purpose of the parting powder. ______________________

____ 1 0 (*c*) (i) Give **one** piece of protective clothing, apart from gloves, that should be worn while pouring the aluminium.

____ 1 0

(ii) Name a tool that can be used to remove the hot casting from the sand, after it has set.

____ 1 0

(*d*) The aluminium handle and supports can be finished to give a shiny, silver appearance.

(i) Describe **one** method of how this finish can be produced.

____

____ 1 0

(ii) Suggest why the base should be painted before assembly.

____

____ 1 0

3. A thermoplastic holder for a personal stereo is shown in the sketch below.

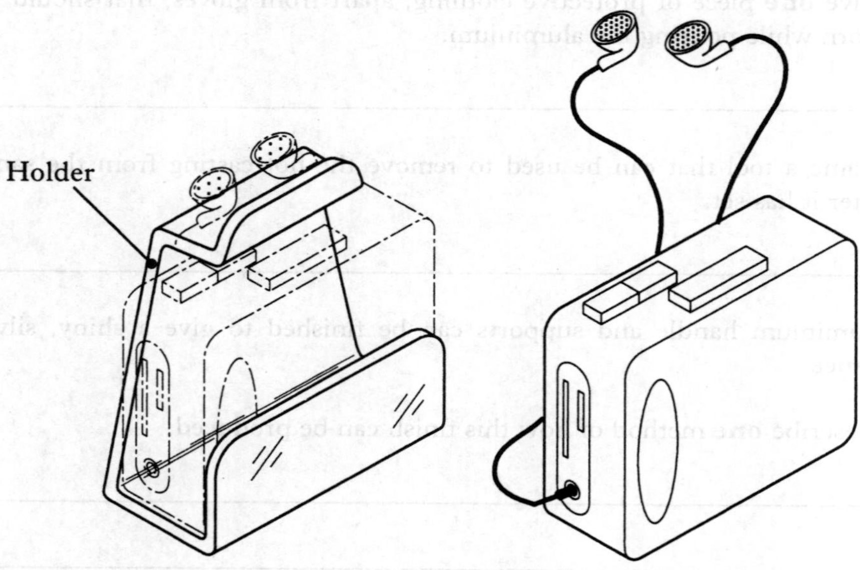

(*a*) Write down **two** statements that should appear in the design specification.

1. The holder must ______________________________ 1 0

2. The holder must ______________________________ 1 0

(*b*) At the investigation stage, the material for the holder and the dimensions of the personal stereo should be considered. Give **one** other aspect that should be investigated.

____

____ 1 0

(*c*) (i) Explain the term "plastic memory".

____ 1 0

(ii) Name a suitable thermoplastic for the personal stereo holder.

____ 1 0

(iii) State a property of the material that makes it a suitable choice for the personal stereo holder.

____ 1 0

(*d*) The main dimensions of a personal stereo are shown in the sketch.

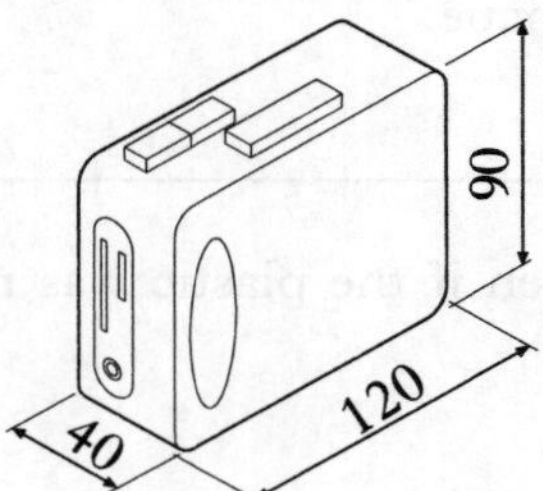

The flat development or net (with three dimensions missing) is shown below.

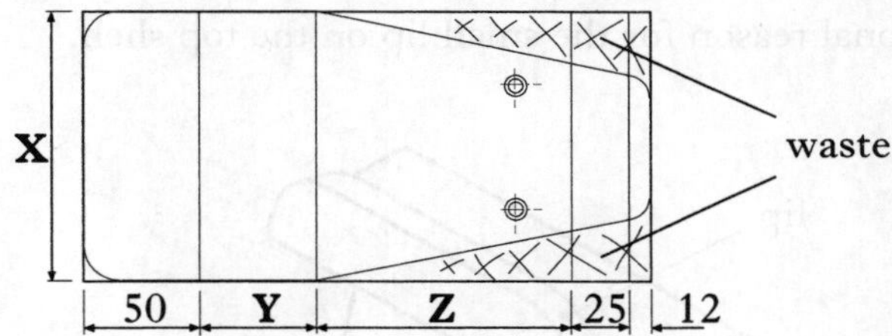

Give a dimension for:

(i) **X** if it is the same length as the stereo ________ mm 1 0

(ii) **Y** if the stereo needs 5 mm clearance ________ mm 1 0

(iii) **Z** if the stereo needs between 15 and 20 mm clearance ________ mm. 1 0

(*e*) (i) Name the **hand tool** used to cut off most of the plastic waste.

____ 1 0

(ii) Name the **hand tool** used to round off the sharp corners.

____ 1 0

(*f*) (i) Explain why the fixing hole has to be countersunk.

____ 1 0

(ii) Sketch a countersink drill.

1 0

(*g*) (i) Name a machine that would heat the plastic along the bend lines to allow it to be formed into shape.

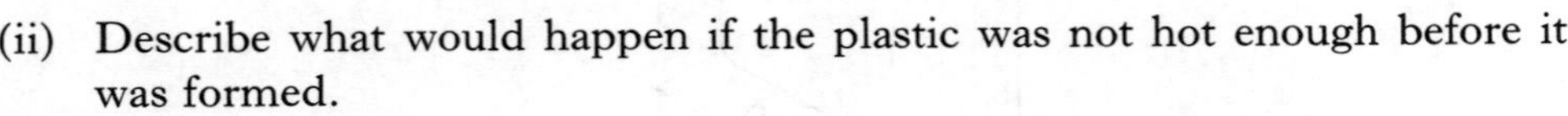

1 0

(ii) Describe what would happen if the plastic was not hot enough before it was formed.

1 0

(*h*) Give a functional reason for the small lip on the top shelf.

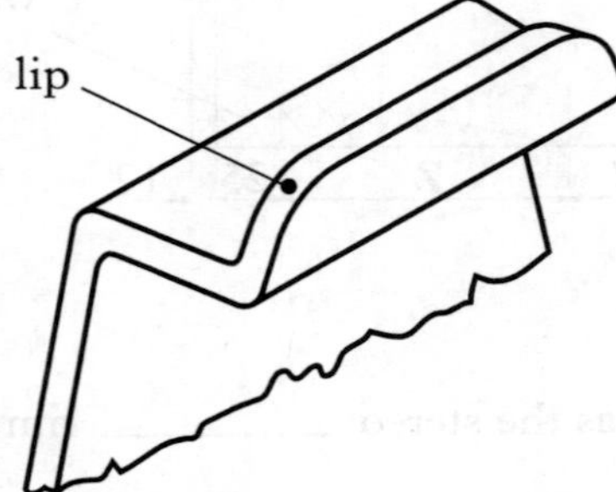

1 0

4. (*a*) (i) Explain what is meant by the term "ergonome".

1 0

(ii) Give an example of the use of an ergonome.

1 0

(*b*) Anthropometrics is concerned with human dimensions. What are the following terms concerned with?

(i) Ergonomics is concerned with

1 0

(ii) Aesthetics is concerned with

1 0

(iii) Function is concerned with

1 0

(iv) Economics is concerned with

1 0

(*c*) Give an example of where anthropometric data can be found.

1 0

5. A table which can be adjusted in height is shown below.

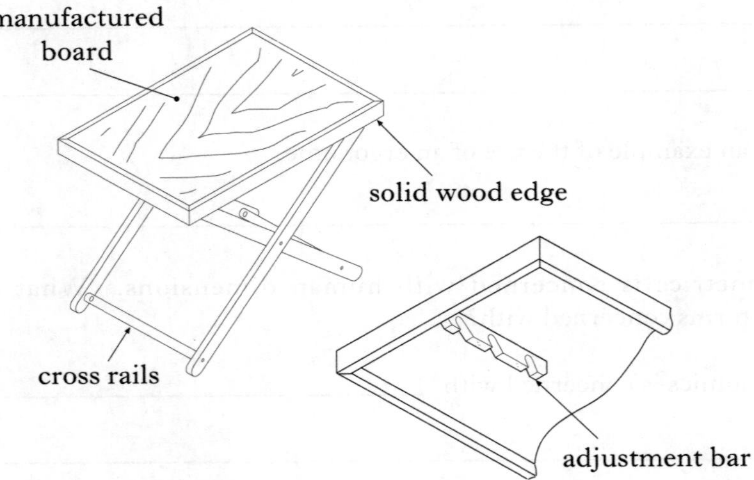

(*a*) Suggest a use for the table when adjusted:

(i) to its top height of 720 mm; ______________________ 1 0

(ii) to its lowest height of 350 mm. ______________________ 1 0

(*b*) The table top is made from a manufactured board with a veneered surface and a solid wood edge.

(i) Name a suitable manufactured board. ______________________ 1 0

(ii) Give a brief description of this board. You can use a sketch to illustrate your answer.

____

____

____

____

______________________ 2 1 0

(iii) Give **two** advantages a manufactured board has over a traditional solid wood top.

1. ______________________ 1 0

2. ______________________ 1 0

(*c*) The adjustment bar which sits on the underside of the table is shown below.

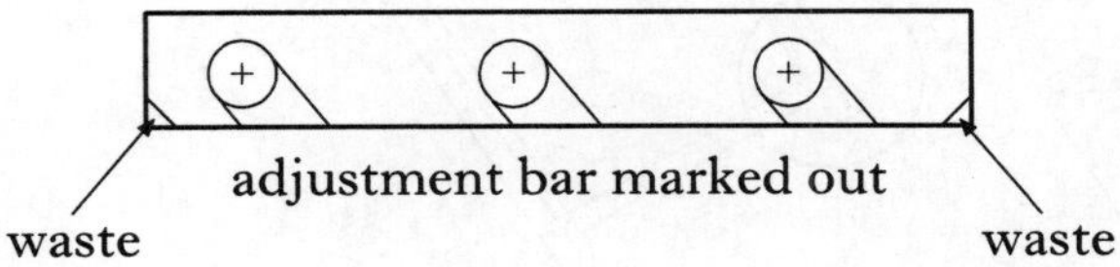

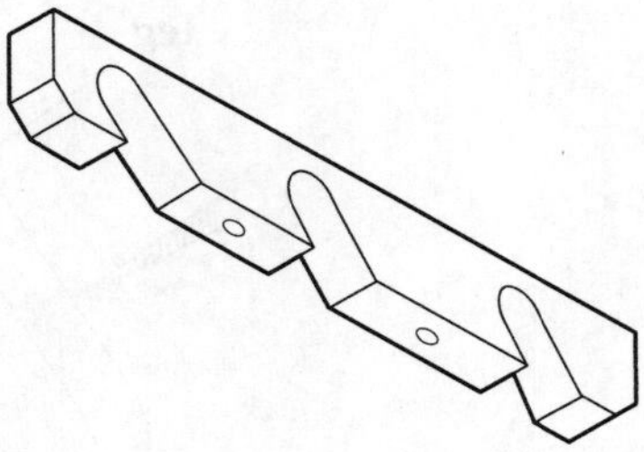

(i) Name the marking out tool which can be used when drawing the sloping lines with a pencil.

____ 1 0

(ii) Describe how you could mark out the adjustment bar.

____

____

____

____ 2 1 0

(iii) Name the hand tool which will cut most of the waste from the two corners.

____ 1 0

(*d*) The adjustment bar is held in position by glueing and screwing.

(i) Name a glue that is supplied ready to use and any excess glue can be removed easily, to prevent staining the wood.

____ 1 0

(ii) The screws are counterbored into the wood. Explain in words and/or with a sketch what is meant by the term counterboring.

____

____

____

________________________ 2 1 0

(*e*)

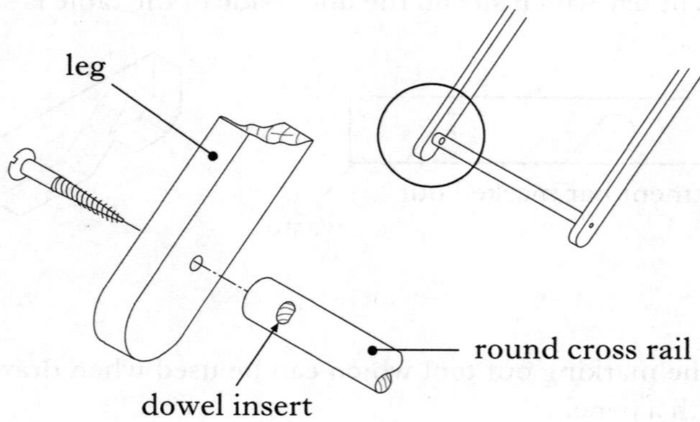

Near each end of the round cross rails, a ∅ 10 mm dowel is glued in place for a functional reason. Explain why this is needed.

____

____

____

____ 1 0

[*END OF QUESTION PAPER*]

SCOTTISH CERTIFICATE OF EDUCATION 1998

MONDAY, 25 MAY
G/C 9.15 AM –10.15 AM
F/**G** 10.15 AM –11.15 AM

CRAFT AND DESIGN STANDARD GRADE

General Level

ATTEMPT ALL QUESTIONS

1. The "Shrimp" table lamp which operates on a low energy bulb is shown.

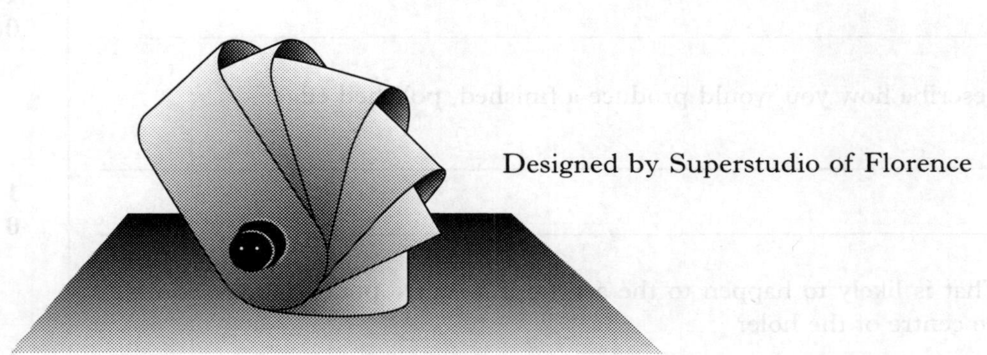

Designed by Superstudio of Florence

(*a*) A design which tries to reproduce a similar lamp starts off with one of the layers as a flat piece of acrylic marked as shown.

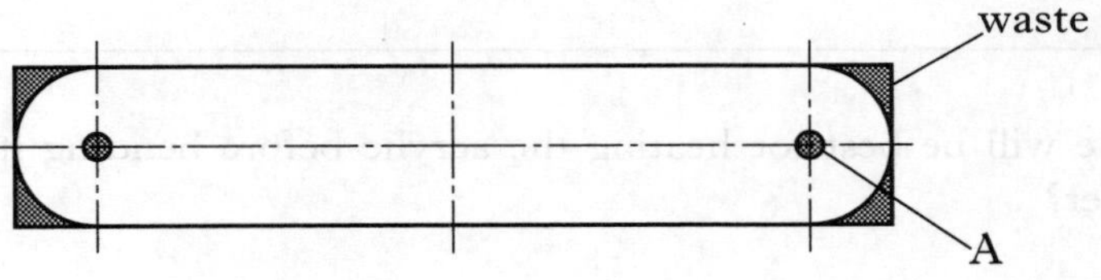

Describe **two** methods of marking out the curved ends on the acrylic.

Method 1 ____

____ **1** **0**

Method 2 ____

____ **1** **0**

(*b*) After marking out, the ends of the acrylic are cut to shape.

(i) Name a hand tool used to remove most of the waste.

____ 1 0

(ii) Describe how to remove the rest of the waste to form a semi-circle.

____

____

____ 1 0

(iii) Describe how you would produce a finished, polished edge.

____

____ 1 0

(*c*) (i) What is likely to happen to the acrylic if a centre punch is used to mark the centre of the hole?

____ 1 0

(ii) It was necessary to drill a "pilot hole" at A. What is the purpose of the pilot hole?

____ 1 0

(*d*) Which machine will be best for heating the acrylic before bending it to shape around a former?

____ 1 0

(*e*) In the forming process, the temperature of the acrylic is important. Describe what might happen if the temperature is

(i) not hot enough ____________________________ 1 0

(ii) too hot. ____________________________ 1 0

2. A laundry box made from Red Pine is shown.

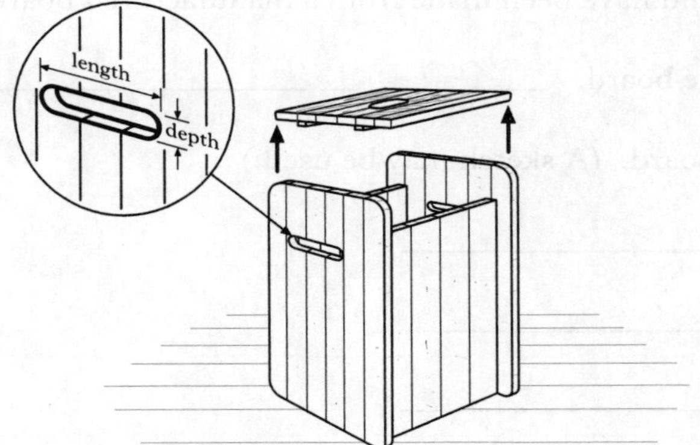

(*a*) The sides are made by joining strips of red pine together and holding them as shown below.

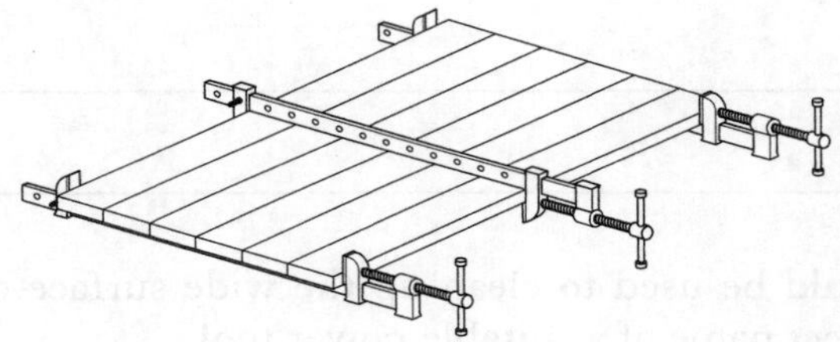

(i) Name the type of joint used. ______________ 1 0

(ii) Give the name of the holding device. ______________ 1 0

(iii) Explain why one holding device is placed on top. ______________

______________ 1 0

(iv) When the holding device is tightened, it could damage the edge of the board. Suggest how this damage could be avoided.

____

______________ 1 0

(*b*) (i) How can you check for "winding"? ______________

______________ 1 0

(ii) Name a tool you can use for this check. ______________

______________ 1 0

(*c*) The laundry box could have been made from a manufactured board.

(i) Name a suitable board. ______________________________ 1 0

(ii) Describe this board. (A sketch may be used.)

____

____

____

______________________ 2 1 0

(iii) Using a manufactured board for the laundry box may save preparation time and may cost less. Give **one** other advantage of using a manufactured board.

____

______________________________ 1 0

(*d*) A portable power tool could be used to clean up the wide surface of the red pine board. Give the correct name of a suitable power tool.

______________________________ 1 0

(*e*) Two slots were cut into the **sides** of the box.

(i) Suggest a purpose for these slots.

____

______________________________ 1 0

(ii) Which factors influence the size of the

length of the slot ______________________________ 1 0

depth of the slot? ______________________________ 1 0

3. A photo frame, made of aluminium and plastic, is shown below.

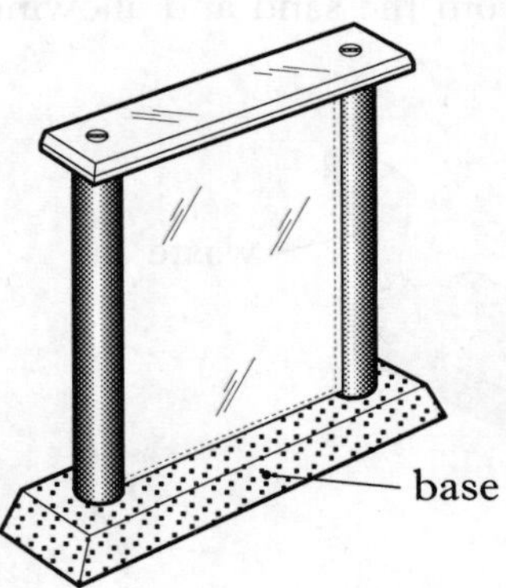

(*a*) The base is made by a process of pouring molten aluminium into a hollow space left in the sand after the wooden pattern was removed.

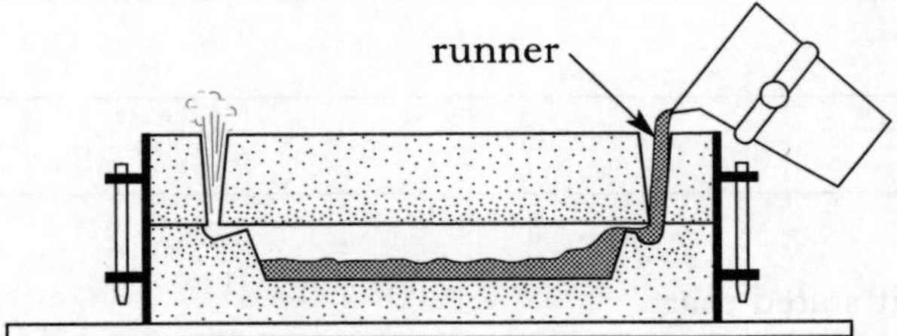

(i) Name this process. ____________________________ **1 0**

(ii) The molten metal is poured down an opening called the "runner". What do you call the opening where the gas escapes and the excess metal appears?

____________________________ **1 0**

(*b*) When pouring the hot metal, gloves and a facemask are used for protection.

Name **one** other piece of clothing that should be worn as protection when pouring molten metal.

____________________________ **1 0**

(*c*) Name a tool that can be used to remove the hot metal from the sand.

____________________________ **1 0**

(*d*) After removing the hot metal from the sand and allowing it to cool, the waste has to be removed.

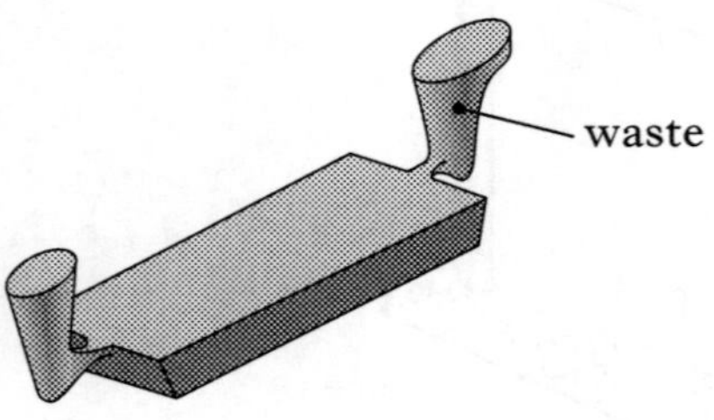

Describe how to remove the waste and how to make the ends smooth.

____

____

____ **2**

____ **1** **0**

(*e*) In the specification it stated that

"The photo frame should not topple over".

Suggest what should have been written into the evaluation to say how well the design met this particular part of this specification.

____

____

____

____ **1**

____ **0**

4. A drawing of a paper weight is shown.

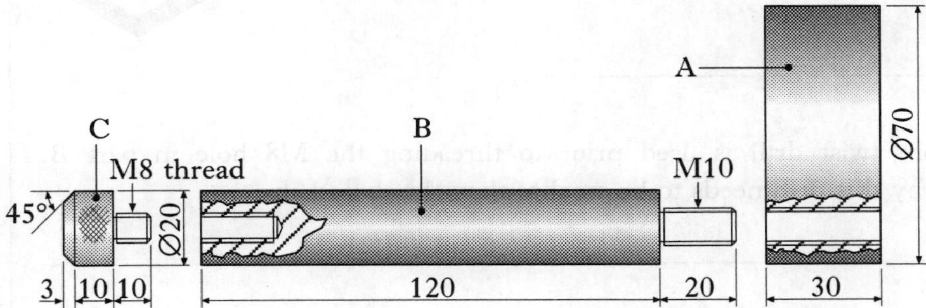

(*a*) A complete cutting list is given.

Part	*Quantity*	*Dimensions*	*Materials*
A	1	Ø70 × 30	Aluminium
B	1	Ø20 × 140	M.S.
C	1	Ø20 × 60	Aluminium

(i) What is the full name of the material used for part B?

____ 1 0

(ii) The length of part C is 60 mm long in the cutting list but yet the finished size is only 23 mm. Suggest a reason for this.

____

____ 1 0

(*b*) In metal turning, what do you call the process

(i) of reducing the diameter, as shown

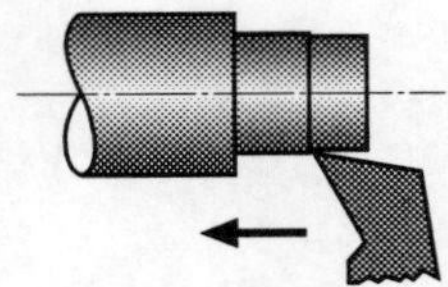

________________________________ 1 0

(ii) of adding texture to the surface?

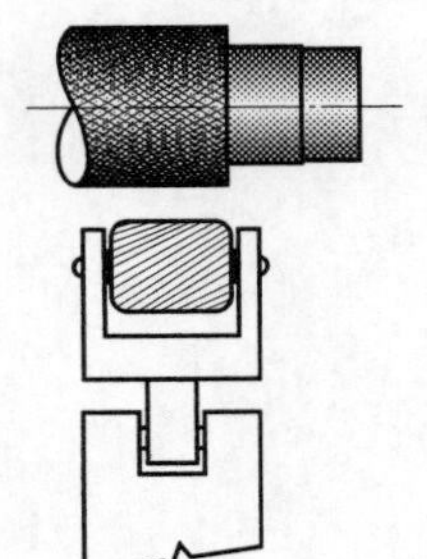

________________________________ 1 0

(*c*) Name the type of drill shown below.

________________________________ 1 0

(*d*) A Ø6·8 mm twist drill is used prior to threading the M8 hole in part B. Suggest why this drill needs to be smaller than the thread size.

____

____ 1 0

(*e*) Complete the sequence of operations for making part C.

Step 1 Face off the end of the bar.

Step 2 Reduce to diameter __________ mm for a distance of 10 mm. 1 0

Step 3 ____ . 1 0

Step 4 Part off to the required length.

Step 5 Hold reduced diameter in chuck, face off and then ______________ . 1 0

5. A clock is shown.

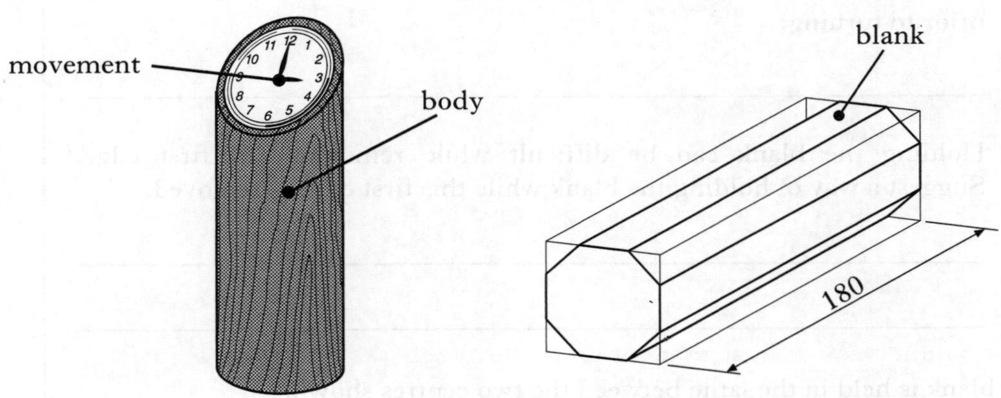

(*a*) The body is made from a close grained hardwood.

Suggest a suitable timber. ______________________ **1 0**

(*b*) If the finished size of the clock is to be 120 × Ø50 mm, suggest **two** reasons why the length of the block is 180 mm.

(i) ______________________________

______________________________ **1 0**

(ii) ______________________________

______________________________ **1 0**

(*c*) The ends of the blank should be prepared before the corners are removed and prior to fitting on the lathe. Describe, in sequence, how the ends should be prepared so that they will fit on the lathe between centres. (Sketches can be used.)

____

____

____

____

____

____

______________________________ **2 1 0**

(*d*) (i) Name a hand tool that can be used to remove the corners from the blank prior to turning.

____ 1 0

(ii) Holding the blank can be difficult while removing the first edge. Suggest a way of holding the blank while this first edge is removed.

____

____ 1 0

(*e*) The blank is held in the lathe between the two centres shown.

(i) Write the correct name under each diagram.

Name ____________________ Name ____________________ 2 1 0

(ii) Which centre must be used in the headstock? ____________________ 1 0

(*f*) (i) Write down a safety check you should carry out on the tailstock.

____ 1 0

(ii) If one end of the wooden blank starts to overheat, what can you do to reduce the risk of this happening again?

____

____ 1 0

6. The "Juicy Salif" Lemon Squeezer is shown.

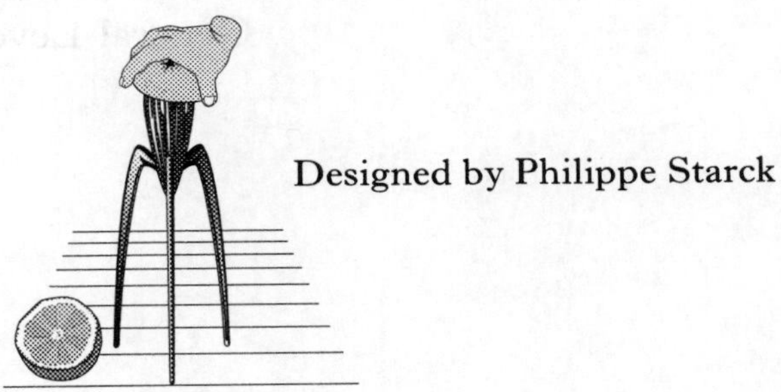

Designed by Philippe Starck

(*a*) In a specification for the squeezer, aluminium could have been chosen as it "must be light in weight". Give **two** other aspects of the specification which would support aluminium as a suitable material for the project.

(i) It must ________________________________ 1

________________________________ 0

(ii) It must ________________________________ 1

________________________________ 0

(*b*) During the investigation and research, some factors which may have influenced the design were identified as

Function *Safety* *Materials* *Size and weight*
Maintenance *Appearance* *Ergonomics* *Anthropometrics* *Cost.*

From the list, which one of these would be mainly concerned with each of the following?

(i) Sharp corners and edges ________________________________ 1 0

(ii) Aesthetic effects ________________________________ 1 0

(iii) Few repairs ________________________________ 1 0

(iv) Fitting your hand ________________________________ 1 0

(*c*) The juice squeezer is quite stable. What is it about the design that makes it stable?

________________________________ 1 0

(*d*) The juice squeezer is "tall". Can you suggest a reason for this?

________________________________ 1 0

[*END OF QUESTION PAPER*]

SCOTTISH CERTIFICATE OF EDUCATION 1999

TUESDAY, 25 MAY
G/C 9.20 AM – 10.20 AM
F/**G** 10.20 AM – 11.20 AM

CRAFT AND DESIGN STANDARD GRADE

General Level

1 Answer all the questions.

2 Read every question carefully before you answer.

3 Write your answers in the spaces provided.

4 Do **not** write in the margins.

5 All dimensions are given in millimetres.

6 Before leaving the examination room you must give this book to the invigilator. If you do not, you may lose all the marks for this paper.

1999

ATTEMPT ALL QUESTIONS

1. A magazine rack is shown.

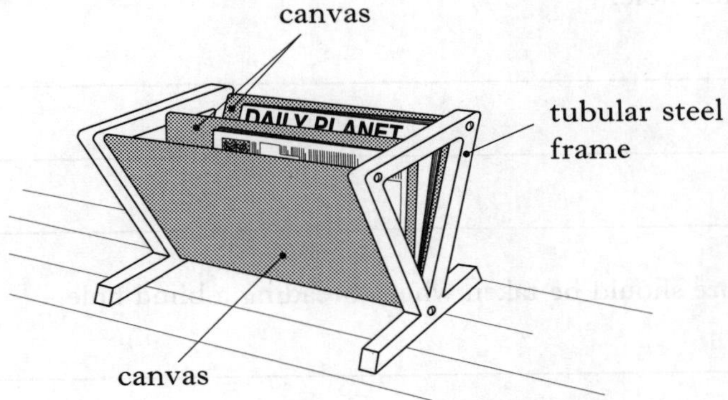

(*a*) Why would the designer produce a presentation drawing of the magazine rack?

____ 1 0

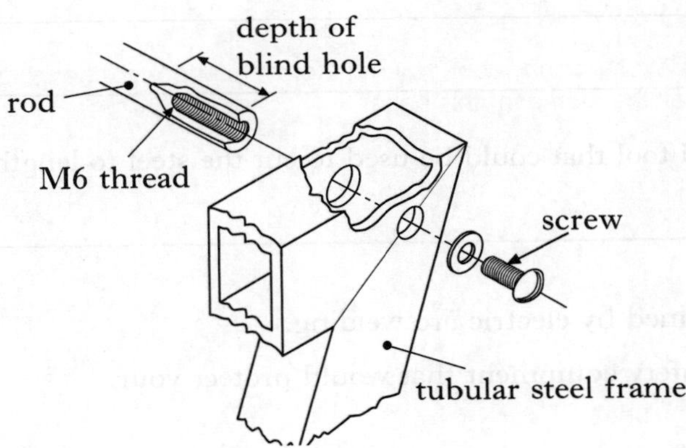

(*b*) During the manufacture, the rods are drilled and threaded.

(i) Name the tool shown which is used to start the drilling process.

Name ______________________ 1 0

(ii) A drill is held in the tailstock chuck for drilling the blind hole. Explain how the correct depth of the blind hole is achieved by using the tailstock.

____

____

____ 1 0

(iii) A thread is cut in the holes after drilling. Describe how the M6 thread is cut into the blind hole.

____

____ 2 1 0

____

(iv) Explain why care should be taken when threading a blind hole.

____

____ 1 0

(*c*) The frame is made from 25 mm square tubular steel.

(i) Give a reason why this material was selected.

____

____ 1 0

(ii) Name a hand tool that could be used to cut the steel to length.

____ 1 0

(*d*) The corners are joined by electric arc welding.

Name a piece of safety equipment that would protect your:

clothes from sparks ________________________ 1 0

eyes. ______________________________ 1 0

(*e*) Write a sequence of operations for preparing and painting the metal frame.

____

____ 2 1 0

____

(*f*) Explain why the frame is painted before its final assembly with the canvas divisions.

____

____ 1 0

2. A flower vase is shown.

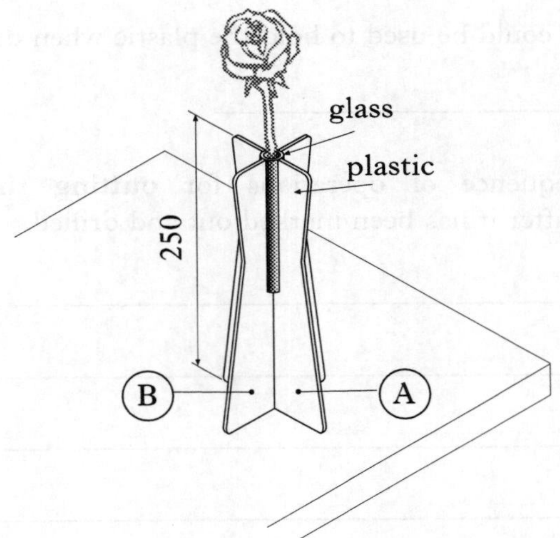

(*a*) Name a suitable type of plastic for (A) and (B). ____________ 1 0

(*b*) Suggest **two** statements which might appear in the design specification for the vase.

1 ________________________________ 1 0

2 ________________________________ 1 0

(*c*) Component (A) is shown marked out below.

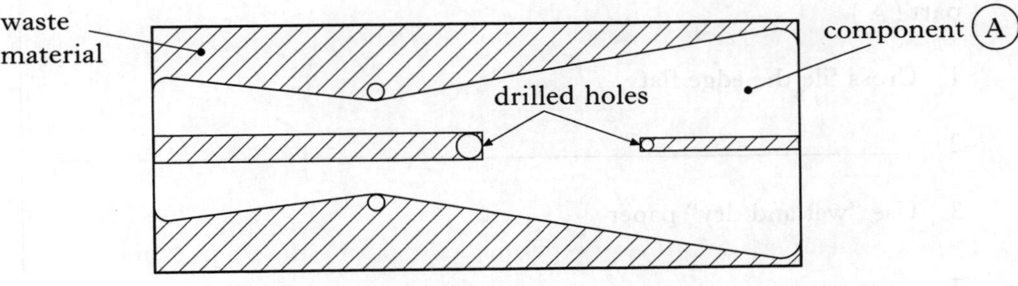

(i) Explain why the bottom of each slot has a drilled hole.

____

____

________________________________ 1 0

(ii) Name a suitable type of drill for drilling these holes.

________________ 1 0

(iii) Name a tool that could be used to hold the plastic when drilling.

______________________________ 1 0

(iv) Write out a sequence of operations for **cutting the outline** of component (A) after it has been marked out and drilled.

____

____

____

____

____

______________________________ 2 1 0

(v) Explain how the surface of the component (A) can be protected from being scratched during manufacture.

____

______________________________ 1 0

(vi) Complete the sequence of operations required to finish the edge of part (A).

1 Cross file the edge flat

2 ______________________________ 1 0

3 Use "wet and dry" paper

4 ______________________________ 1 0

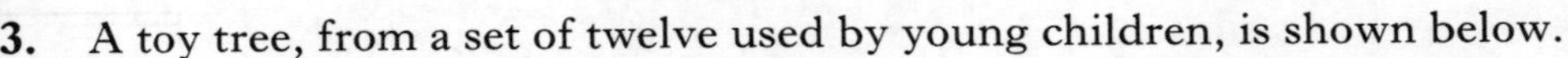

3. A toy tree, from a set of twelve used by young children, is shown below.

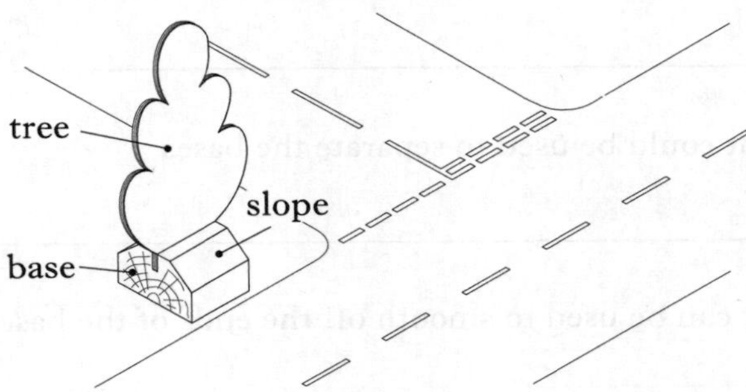

(*a*) Name a thin multi-layered manufactured board suitable for making the toy trees.

______________________ 1 0

(*b*) (i) Name a machine that can be used to cut around the shape of the trees.

______________________ 1 0

(ii) Give a safety precaution that should be observed while using this machine.

____

______________________ 1 0

(*c*) Complete the following statement which might appear in the design specification for the tree.

Because the tree is for a young child, the finish must ______________________

______________________ 1 0

(*d*) In making a set, all the bases are marked out at the same time as shown.

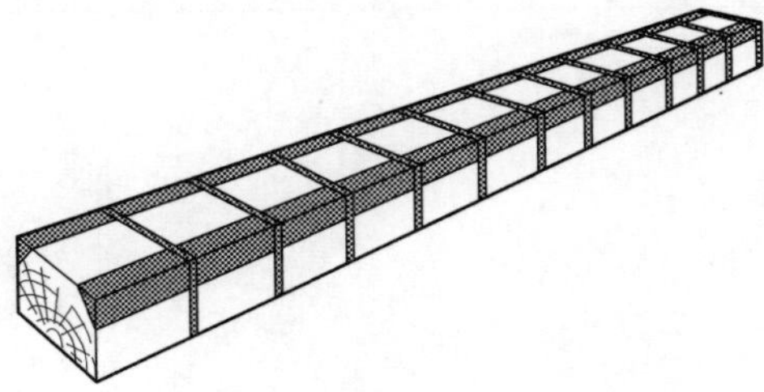

(i) Name the marking out tool used to accurately mark the lines around the timber with a pencil.

______________________ 1 0

(ii) Name a hand tool that could be used to cut the slope on the edges.

____ **1** **0**

(iii) Name a hand saw that could be used to separate the bases.

____ **1** **0**

(iv) Name a machine that can be used to smooth off the ends of the base after they have been sawn.

____ **1** **0**

(*e*) Name a suitable finish for the toy tree and base.

____ **1** **0**

4. Information taken from a booklet on ergonomics and anthropometrics is given below. Give an example of an object where a designer may have used this data.

(*a*) Stature

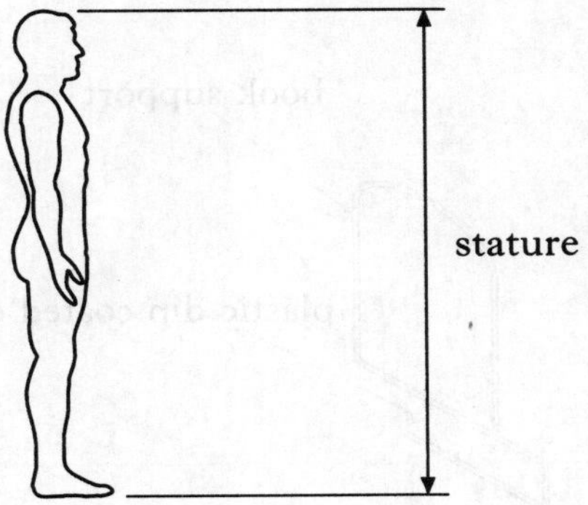

Object ____________________ **1 0**

(*b*) Popliteal Height

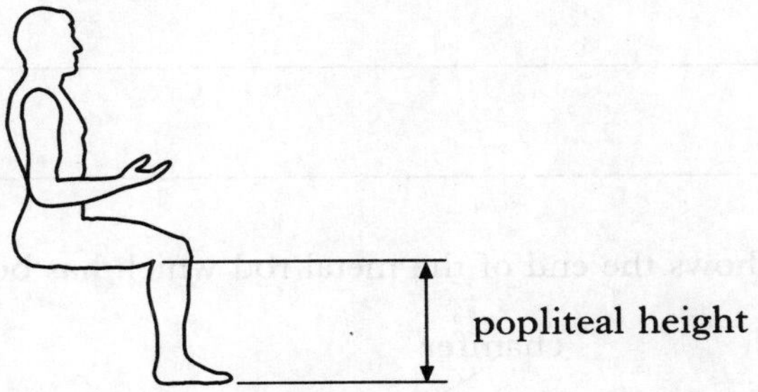

Object ____________________ **1 0**

(*c*) Grip

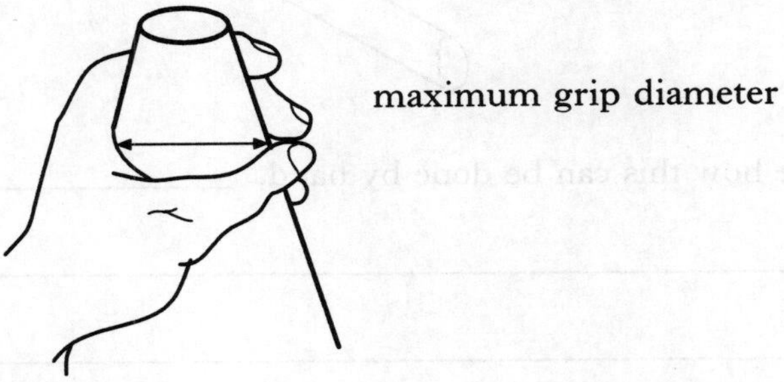

Object ____________________ **1 0**

5. A book support, which is made from wire, is shown.

book support

plastic dip coated end

(*a*) Give **two** factors relating to the books which would have to be considered prior to writing the design specification for the book support.

(i) ______________________________ 1 0

(ii) ______________________________ 1 0

(*b*) The sketch shows the end of the metal rod which has been chamfered.

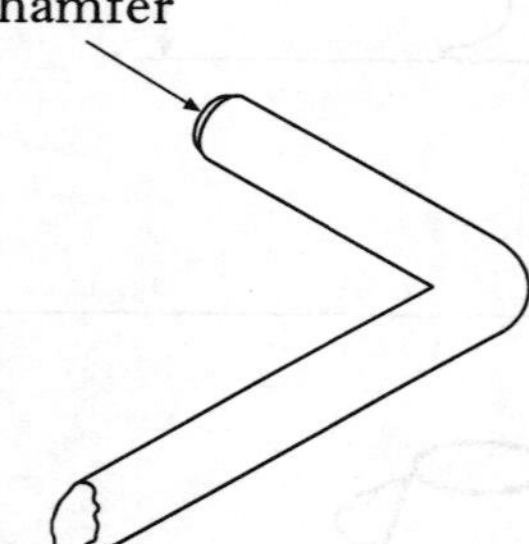

Describe how this can be done by hand. ______________________________

____

______________________________ 1 0

(*c*) The end is bent to a right angle. Why?

____

______________________________ 1 0

6. Initial ideas for a collapsible drawing table are shown below.

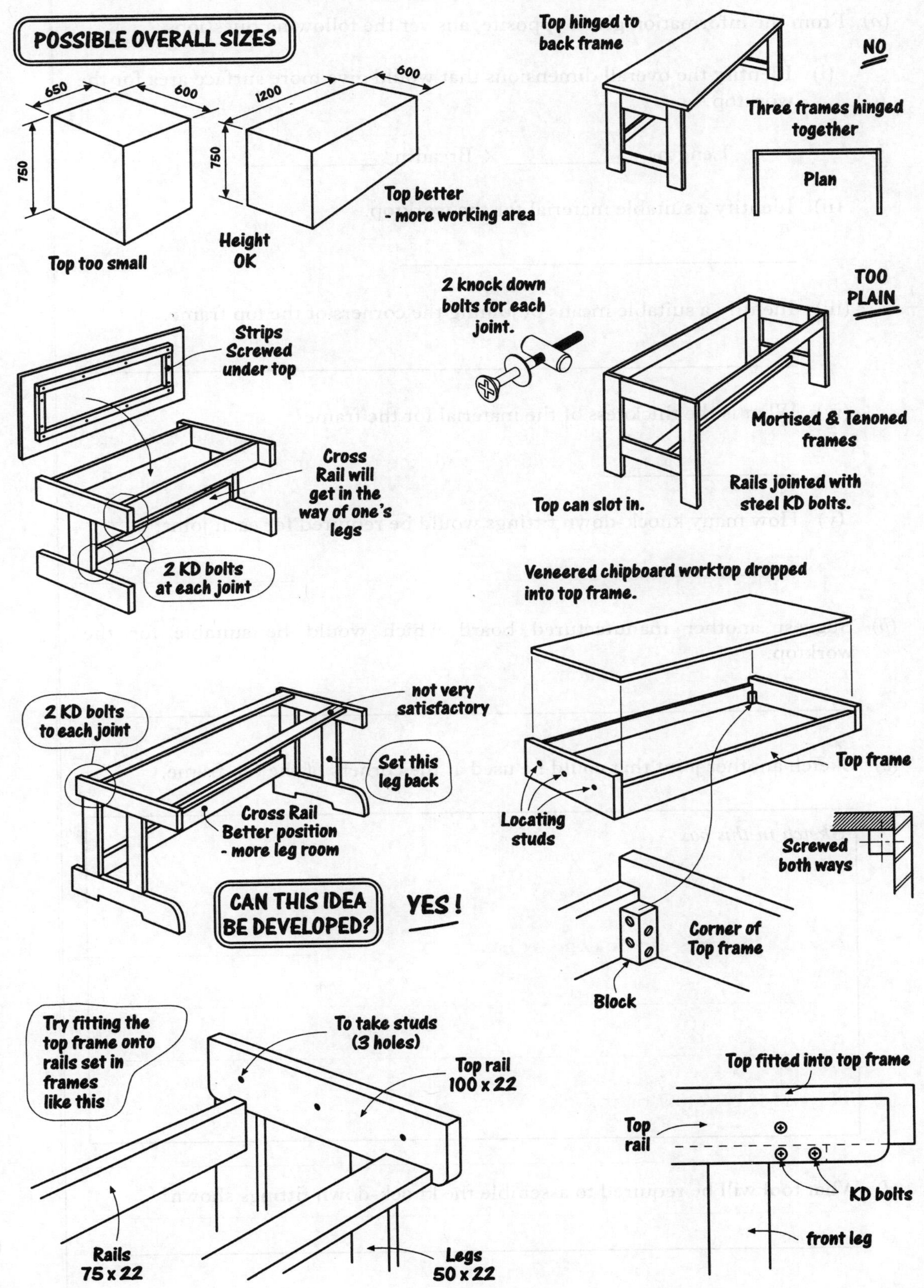
POSSIBLE OVERALL SIZES
650
600
750
1200
600
750
Top too small
Height OK
Top better - more working area
Top hinged to back frame
NO
Three frames hinged together
Plan
2 knock down bolts for each joint.
TOO PLAIN
Strips Screwed under top
Mortised & Tenoned frames
Cross Rail will get in the way of one's legs
Top can slot in.
Rails jointed with steel KD bolts.
2 KD bolts at each joint
Veneered chipboard worktop dropped into top frame.
not very satisfactory
2 KD bolts to each joint
Set this leg back
Top frame
Cross Rail Better position - more leg room
Locating studs
Screwed both ways
CAN THIS IDEA BE DEVELOPED?
YES !
Corner of Top frame
Block
Try fitting the top frame onto rails set in frames like this
To take studs (3 holes)
Top rail 100 x 22
Top fitted into top frame
Top rail
KD bolts
front leg
Rails 75 x 22
Legs 50 x 22

(*a*) From the information given opposite, answer the following questions.

(i) Identify the overall dimensions that would give more surface area for the worktop.

Length ____________ × Breadth ____________ 2 1 0

(ii) Identify a suitable material for the worktop.

______________________________ 1 0

(iii) Identify a suitable means of joining the corners of the top frame.

______________________________ 1 0

(iv) What is the thickness of the material for the frame?

______________________________ 1 0

(v) How many knock-down fittings would be required for each joint?

______________________________ 1 0

(*b*) Suggest another manufactured board which would be suitable for the worktop.

______________________________ 1 0

(*c*) Sketch another joint that could be used at the corners of the top frame.

Sketch in this box

1 0

(*d*) What tool will be required to assemble the knock-down fittings shown?

______________________________ 1 0

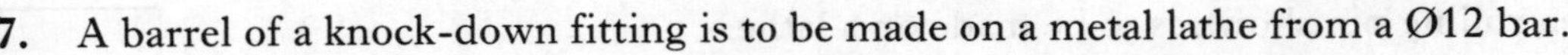

7. A barrel of a knock-down fitting is to be made on a metal lathe from a Ø12 bar.

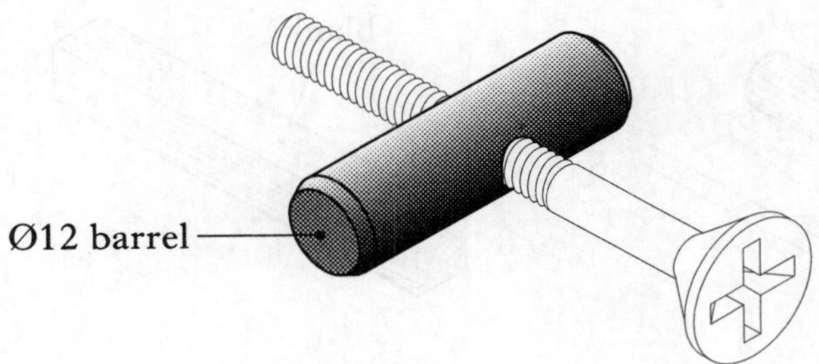

(*a*) Name a lightweight non-ferrous metal that could be used for the barrel.

______________________________ **1 0**

(*b*) The chuck shown below holds the bar on the lathe. Name this chuck.

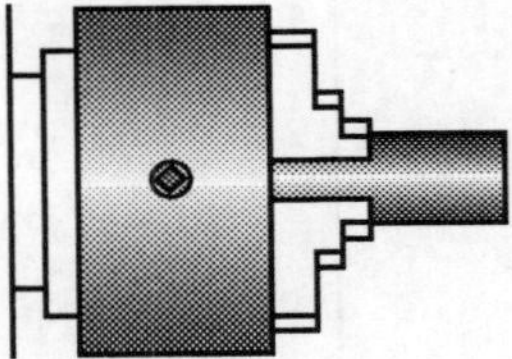

Name ______________________________ **1 0**

(*c*) Name the lathe cutting tool which would cut the barrel from the longer bar while still on the lathe.

______________________________ **1 0**

(*d*) Complete the sequence of operations to turn the barrel to the stage shown below.

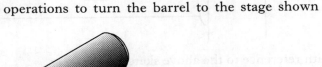

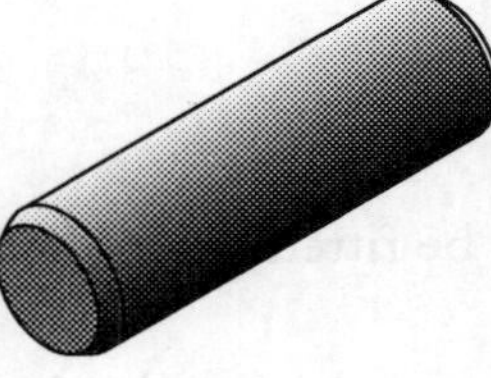

(i) Face off the end of the bar

(ii) ______________________________ **1 0**

(iii) Cut to length

(iv) ______________________________ **1 0**

8. The wooden rolling pin shown is to be made on a lathe.

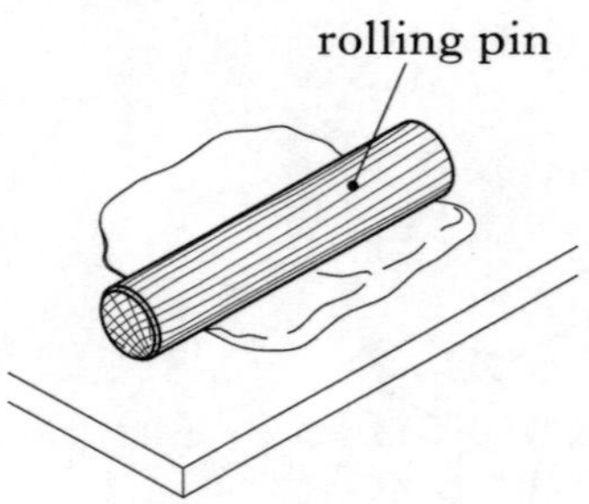

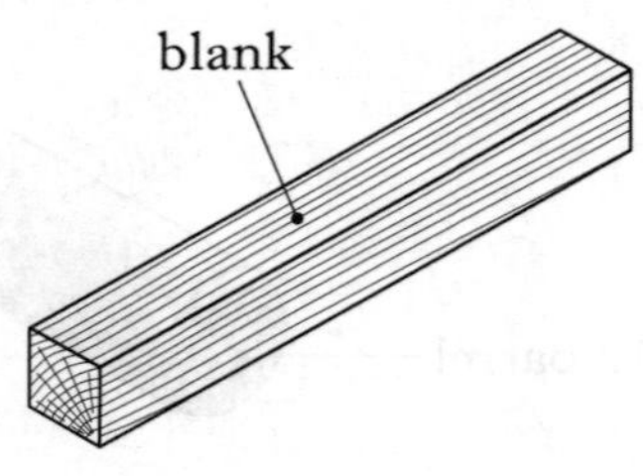

(*a*) Name a close-grained hardwood suitable for turning the rolling pin.

______________________________ 1 0

(*b*) Complete the sequence of operations required to prepare the blank before fitting it onto the lathe.

(i) Mark the diagonals on both ends

(ii) ______________________

(iii) ______________________

(iv) ______________________

(v) ______________________

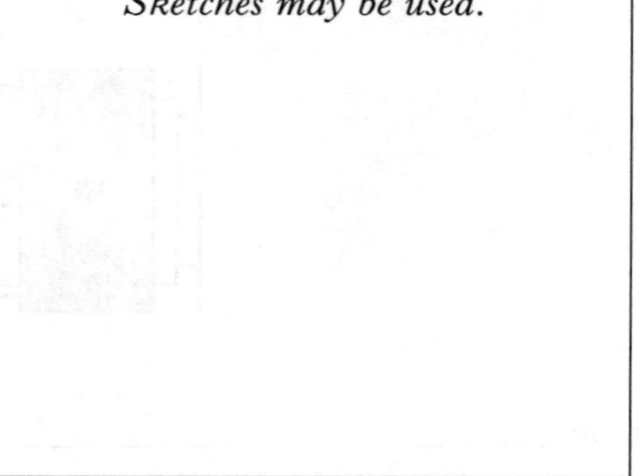

2 1 0

(*c*)

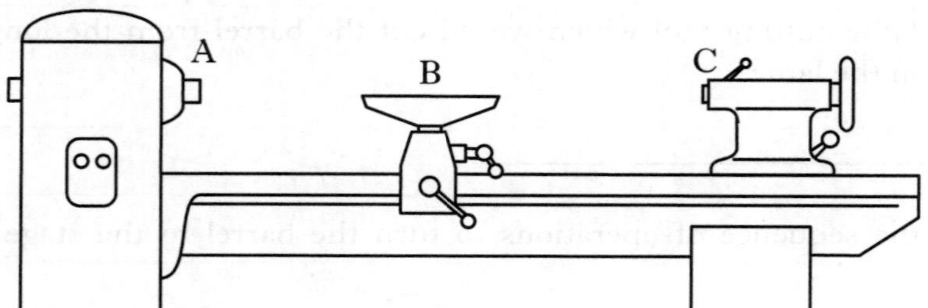

With reference to the above sketch

(i) where would the fork centre be fitted—A, B or C? ________________ 1 0

(ii) where would the revolving centre be fitted—A, B or C? ________________ 1 0

(*d*) Once the woodwork lathe has been set up, but before it is switched on, it is good practice to rotate the blank by hand. Explain why this should be done.

____ 1 0

[*END OF QUESTION PAPER*]

COTTISH
ERTIFICATE OF
DUCATION
994

TUESDAY, 31 MAY
11.40 AM –12.40 PM

CRAFT AND DESIGN
STANDARD GRADE
Credit Level

ATTEMPT ALL QUESTIONS

. Several wall-mounted coat hanger brackets are to be made from acrylic sheet. One is shown below along with a drawing of how it was marked out, prior to bending.

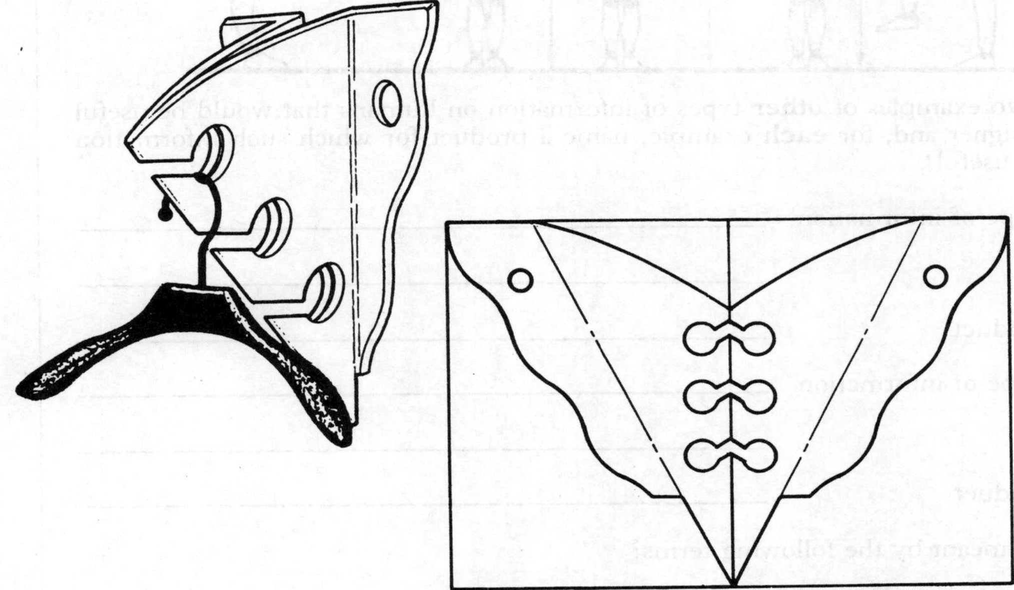

(*a*) Give **two** advantages of using a template to mark the outline of the bracket.

1. ______________________________

____

2. ______________________________

______________________________ 2 1 0

(*b*) What tool is likely to be used to cut out the bracket?

______________________________ 1 0

(*c*) Why is it better to finish and polish all the edges of the acrylic before bending?

____

______________________________ 1 0

(*d*) Name one other material that could be used to make this bracket.

______________________________ 1 0

2. When designing products for human use, designers usually have data on body dimensions but they often require more information about people.

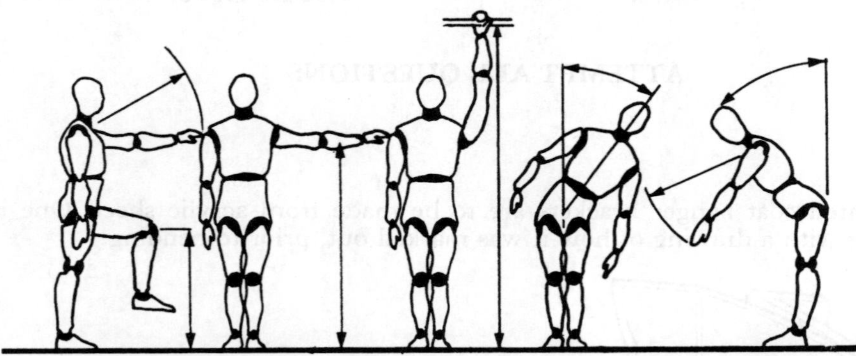

(*a*) Give **two** examples of **other** types of information on humans that would be useful to a designer and, for **each** example, name a product for which such information may be useful.

(i) Type of information ________________________

________________________ 1 0

Product ________________________ 1 0

(ii) Type of information ________________________

________________________ 1 0

Product ________________________ 1 0

(*b*) What is meant by the following terms?

Ergonomics ________________________ 1

________________________ 0

Anthropometrics ________________________ 1

________________________ 0

(*c*) Identify two ergonomic factors which may have influenced the design of this hand held games console.

1. ________________________ 1

________________________ 0

2. ________________________ 1

________________________ 0

Two drawings of a small table are shown below. The table was manufactured from man-made board with a coloured plastic laminate finish.

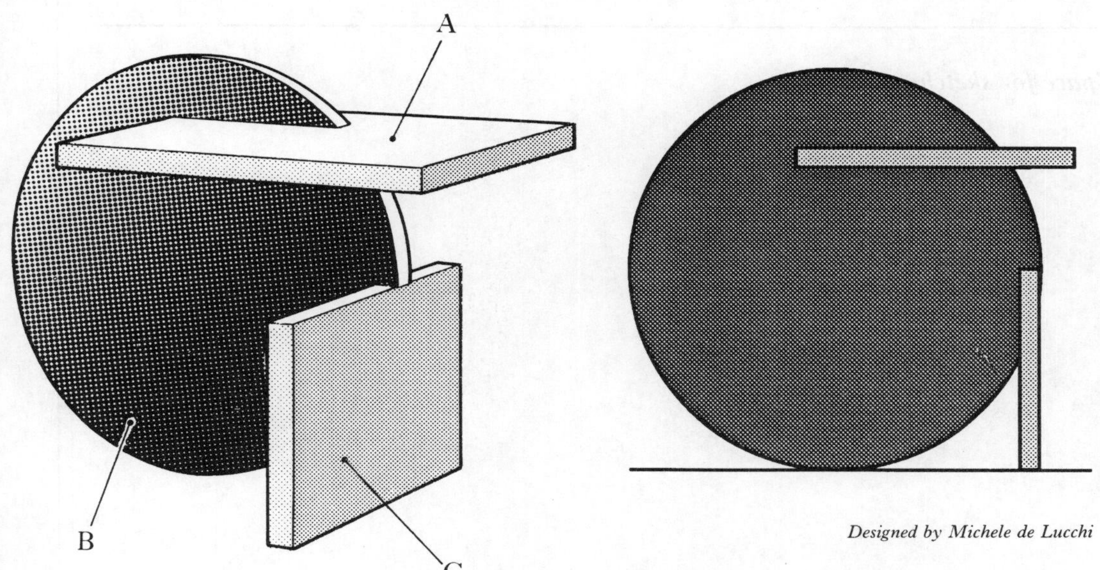

Designed by Michele de Lucchi

(*a*) Describe one method of joining part A to part B. **Use sketches to illustrate your answer.**

____

____

(*Space for sketches*)

2
1
0

(*b*) Describe one method of joining part B to part C. **Use sketches to illustrate your answer.**

____

____

(*Space for sketches*)

2
1
0

(*c*) (i) Give one **functional** advantage of using plastic laminate as a surface finish for the table.

____

____ 1
0

(ii) Give one disadvantage.

____

____ 1
0

Two sketches of a pupil's design for a tape dispenser are shown below.

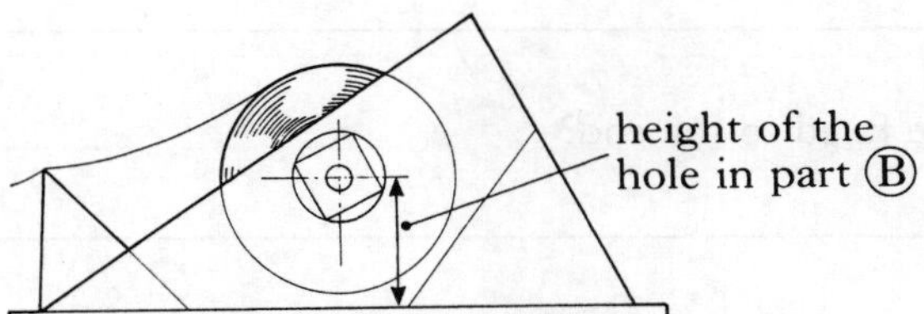

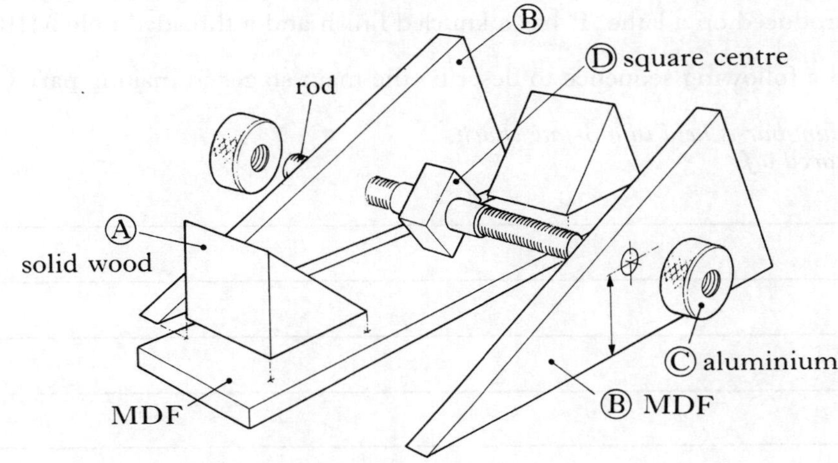

(*a*) Suggest **two** possible methods of fixing part Ⓐ to the base.

1. ____ **1 0**

2. ____ **1 0**

(*b*) (i) What determines the height of the holes in parts Ⓑ?

____ **1 0**

(ii) How would you ensure that these holes were correctly aligned at the drilling stage?

____

____

____

____ **2 1 0**

(*c*) (i) What determines the size of the square centre Ⓓ?

1 0

(ii) Why should this centre **not** be fixed to the rod?

1 0

(*d*) Part Ⓒ is produced on a lathe. It has a knurled finish and a threaded hole M10.

Complete the following sequence to describe the main stages in making part Ⓒ.

The aluminium bar is held in a 3-jaw chuck.
The bar is faced off.

5 4 3 2 1 0

(*e*) In evaluating the product, it was found that the dispenser tended to lift and slip when the tape was pulled.

Suggest **two modifications** that might improve this aspect of the product's performance.

1.

1 0

2.

1 0

5. A design for a portable camping stove is shown below.

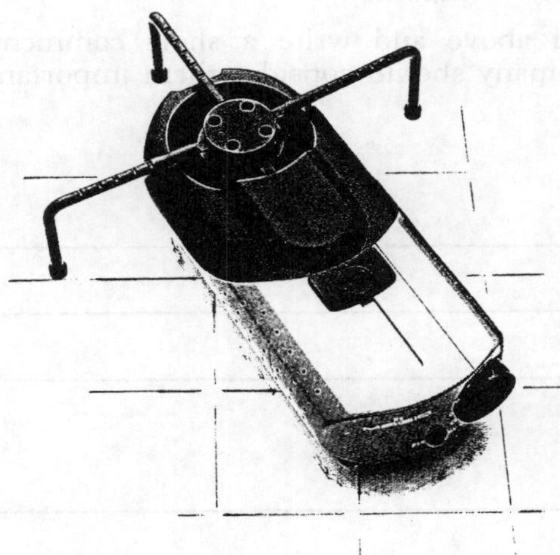

Designed by Young S Kim

Write down **three** things that should be included in the design specification for such a camping stove.

1. ______________________________ **1** **0**

2. ______________________________ **1** **0**

3. ______________________________ **1** **0**

6. A small company, which manufactures toys, has been asked to design a range of pull-along toy animals for Christmas. They will be put on sale in several major toy stores along with toy designs from other companies.

Study the situation described above and write a short comment on **each** of the following, stating why the company should consider them important in designing new toys.

(*a*) *Selection of materials.*

1
0

(*b*) *Cost of the finished product.*

1
0

(*c*) *Aesthetics.*

1
0

(*d*) *Manufacturing techniques.*

1
0

7. A tourist board is planning to build a new adventure playground and picnic area on the outskirts of a small town.

(*a*) Write down **two** aspects that may have a harmful effect on the country environment as a result of people using a playground and picnic site.

1. ________________________________ 1 0

2. ________________________________ 1 0

(*b*) Write down **two** steps that could be taken to prevent or discourage damage to the environment.

1. ________________________________ 1 0

2. ________________________________ 1 0

(*c*) A range of materials is available for use in building the new area. Describe **two** properties a material should have before it could be considered suitable for use in the playground or picnic area.

1. ________________________________ 1 0

2. ________________________________ 1 0

8. A proposed design for a candle holder is shown below.

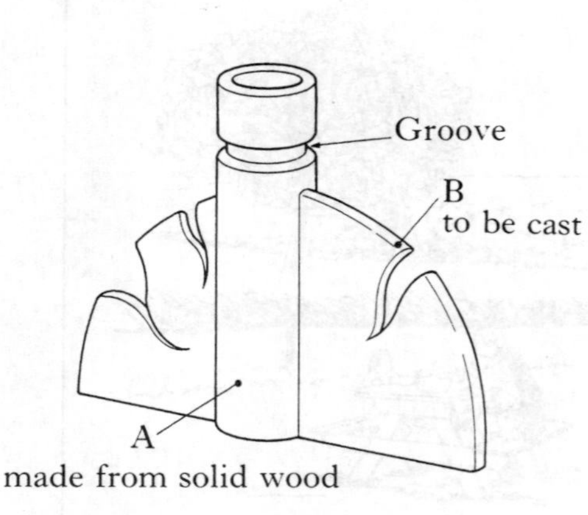

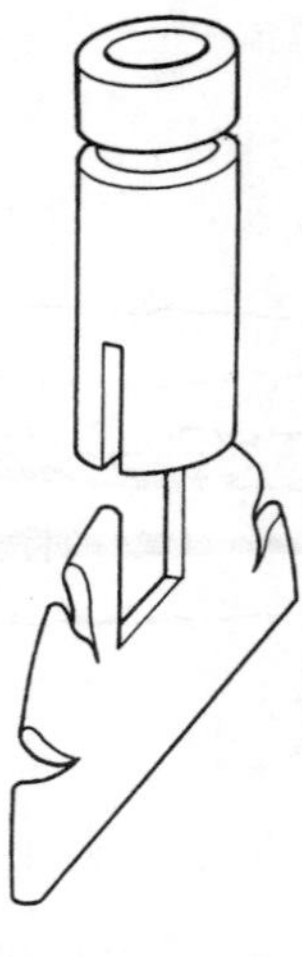

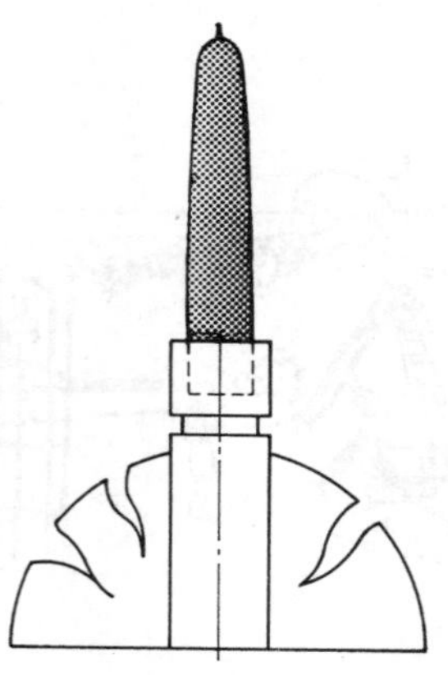

(*a*) Comment on the following aspects.

(i) The choice of materials.

____

____ 1 0

(ii) The stability of the completed candle holder.

____

____ 1 0

(iii) Two possible difficulties in making the candle holder.

1. ____

____ 1 0

2. ____

____ 1 0

(*b*) Write a short note on each of the following casting terms.

Crucible ____

____ 1 0

Runner ____

____ 1 0

Cope and drag ____

____ 1 0

Riser ____

____ 1 0

9. Describe any **three** of the following: *pop-rivetting, plug tap, micrometer, haunched mortise and tenon* and *vacuum forming.*

Your answers should include sketches and comments, explaining **where, how** and **why** the process or tool would be used.

1st choice *Space for sketch*

2
1
0

2nd choice *Space for sketch*

2
1
0

3rd choice *Space for sketch*

2
1
0

[*END OF QUESTION PAPER*]

SCOTTISH CERTIFICATE OF EDUCATION 1995

THURSDAY, 25 MAY
11.40 AM – 12.40 PM

CRAFT AND DESIGN
STANDARD GRADE
Credit Level

ATTEMPT ALL QUESTIONS

1. This toothbrush handle was moulded in plastic.

Designed by Philippe Starck

(*a*) What **two** properties make plastic an appropriate material for toothbrushes?

Property 1 ____

____ 1 0

Property 2 ____

____ 1 0

(*b*) Why do you think the designer shaped the handle in this way?

____

____

____ 1 0

1995

2. The wooden chair below was designed in 1917. Originally it was intended to be mass produced (lots of them were to be made) in craft workshops.

Designed by Gerrit Reitveld

Study the drawing of the chair before answering the following questions.

(*a*) Write down **two** reasons why the design of the chair makes it easy to produce in large numbers.

1. ______________________________________ 1

______________________________________ 0

2. ______________________________________ 1

______________________________________ 0

(*b*) The chair is finished with paint. Give **three** reasons for choosing this finish.

1. ______________________________________ 1

______________________________________ 0

2. ______________________________________ 1

______________________________________ 0

3. ______________________________________ 1

______________________________________ 0

(*c*) If the chair were to be made in your school workshop, suggest a suitable material for each of the following parts and then give a reason for choosing that material. 1

(i) The wooden frame Material ____________________ 0

Reason for choice ____________________________ 1

______________________________________ 0

(ii) The seat and backrest Material ______________________ 1 0

Reason for choice ______________________

______________________ 1 0

3. A pupil's design ideas for a scoring block for a board game is shown below.

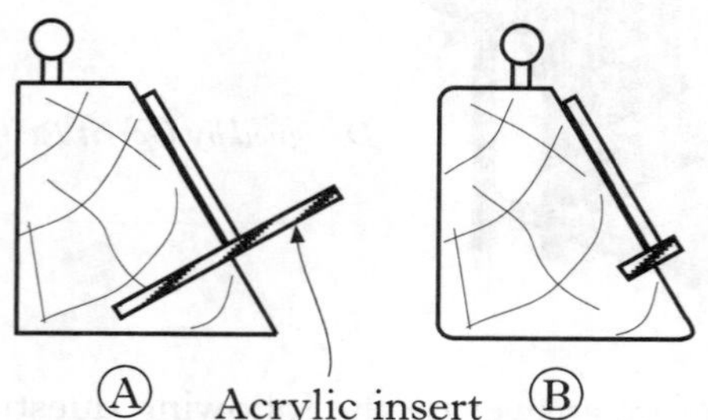

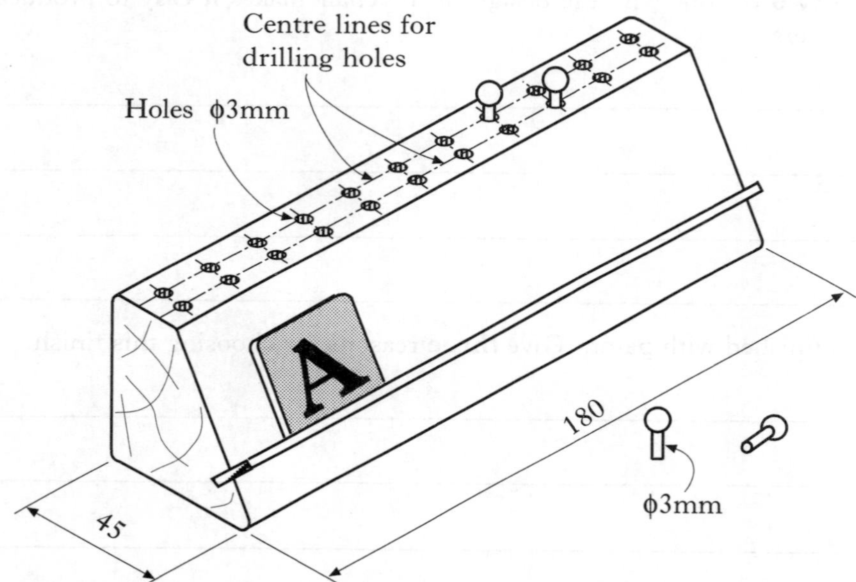

(*a*) Give **two** reasons why design Ⓑ is better than design Ⓐ.

1. ______________________

______________________ 1 0

2. ______________________

______________________ 1 0

(*b*) Which hand tool should be used to mark out the long centre line for each of the two rows of holes?

______________________ 1 0

(*c*) A smoothing plane was used to finish the sloping surface on the block.

(i) Using the diagram of the plane below, explain how to check and adjust the blade before use.

3 2 1 0

(ii) How could you test that the blade was correctly set before using it on the block?

1 0

(iii) Explain the difference between a Jack plane and a smoothing plane.

1 0

(*d*) Using the diagram of the pillar drill, explain how to set the depth of the drill so that all of the holes for the scoring pegs will be 10 mm deep.

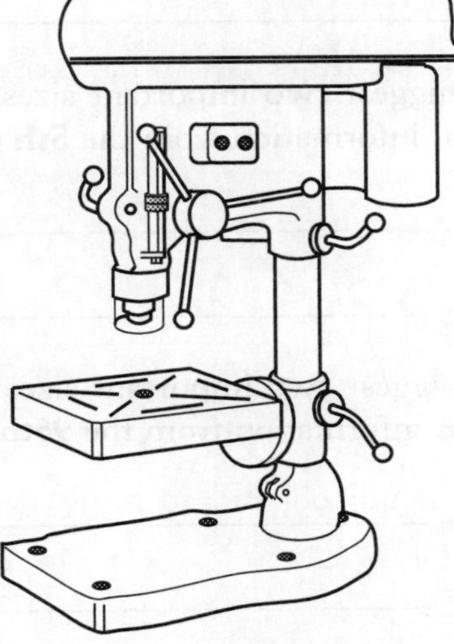

2 1 0

(*e*) Name the **type** of drill that would be used in this machine to drill these holes.

1 0

4. A traditional telephone box is shown below.

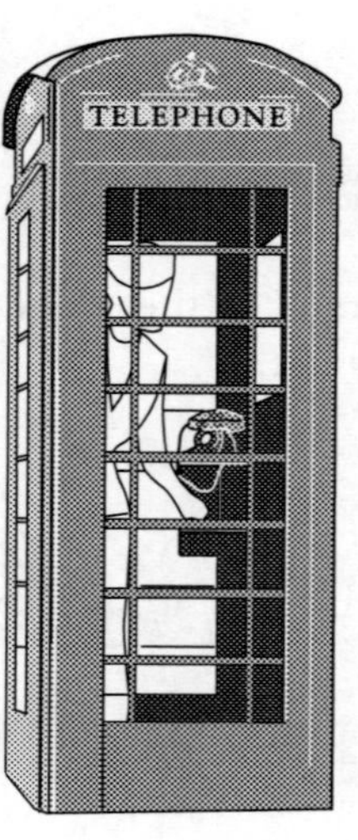

(*a*) Give **two** examples of anthropometric data that would have been required to design this public telephone box so that it could be accessed by everyone in the 5th to 95th percentile range.

1. ____

____ 1 0

2. ____

____ 1 0

(*b*) Write down **one** way this information could be found out other than by measuring a wide range of people.

____ 1 0

(*c*) How could a design using this information be tested to check that it is suitable before making the telephone boxes?

____

____ 1 0

(*d*) (i) Suggest **two** important sizes of the telephone box which would be based on information from the **5th** percentile.

1. ____ 1 0

2. ____ 1 0

(ii) Suggest **two** important sizes of the telephone box which would be based on information from the **95th** percentile.

1. ____ 1 0

2 ____ 1 0

5. Explain the difference between an initial design brief and a design specification. (You may wish to give examples to explain your answer.)

2
1
0

6. Details of a gear stick for a car are shown below along with an exploded and a cross sectional drawing showing how it is assembled.

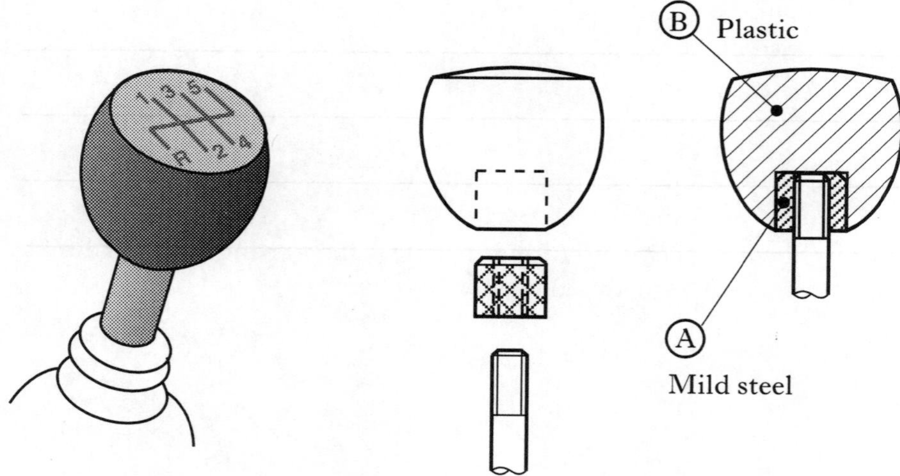

Read the following stages of manufacture used to produce part Ⓐ on the metalwork lathe.

1. Face off
2. Centre drill
3. Drill to the tapping size
4. Tap thread
5. Knurl
6. Chamfer
7. Part off

Answer the following questions.

(*a*) (i) For which of the above stages might the compound slide be set to an angle of 45°?

____________________ **1**
0

(ii) What adjustment should be made to the lathe before knurling?

____

____ **1**
0

(iii) Sketch a parting tool below. 1 0

(iv) Explain how to check the cutting height of the parting tool. (You may wish to use sketches to illustrate your answer.) 2 1 0

(v) What might happen if the parting tool were set below the correct height? 1 0

(*b*) Why has part Ⓐ been knurled? 1 0

(*c*) What is the purpose of the chamfer on part Ⓐ? 1 0

(*d*) Write down **two** pieces of ergonomic information that should be considered before deciding on the

(i) size of part Ⓑ 1 0

(ii) position of the gear stick. 1 0

7. An extract from a pupil's folio is shown below.

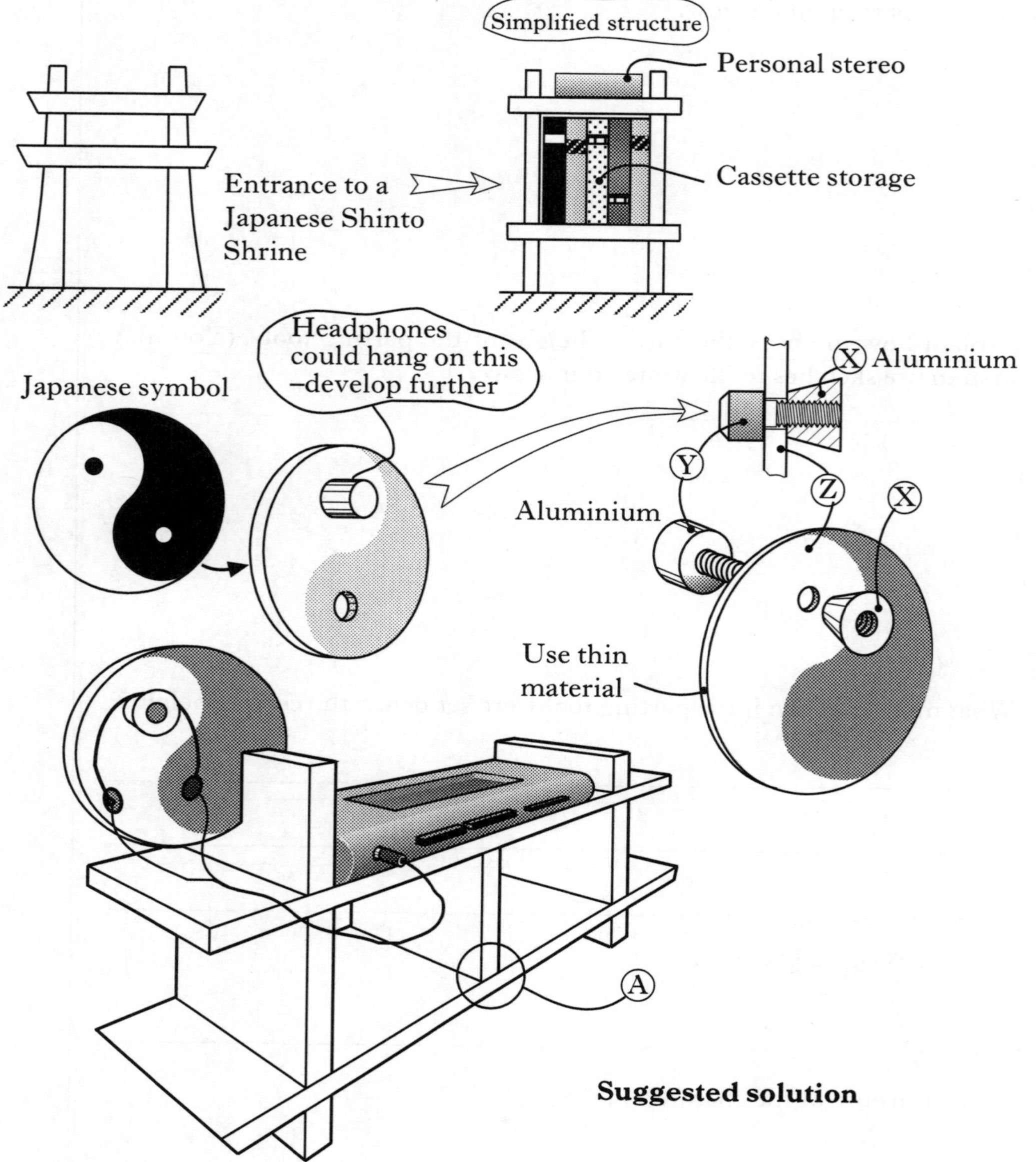

Suggested solution

(*a*) (i) Name a suitable wood joint that could be used at Ⓐ. 1 0

(ii) Give **one** functional and **one** aesthetic reason why this joint was chosen.

Functional reason ________ 1 0

Aesthetic reason ________ 1 0

(*b*) (i) Name a suitable material that could be used to make part Ⓩ.

____________________________________ 1 0

(ii) Give **one** reason why this material was chosen.

____ 1 0

(iii) Suggest **two** ways of obtaining the required colour contrast on this material.

1. ____ 1 0
2. ____ 1 0

(*c*) (i) List in sequence **three** stages in **cutting** the internal thread on part Ⓧ.

1. ________________________________
2. ________________________________
3. ________________________________

3 2 1 0

(ii) What is the functional reason for taper turning part Ⓧ?

____

____ 1 0

(iii) Name **one** other **non ferrous** metal that could be used for part Ⓨ.

____________________________________ 1 0

8. A vacuum formed package for a computer mouse and its accessories is shown below.

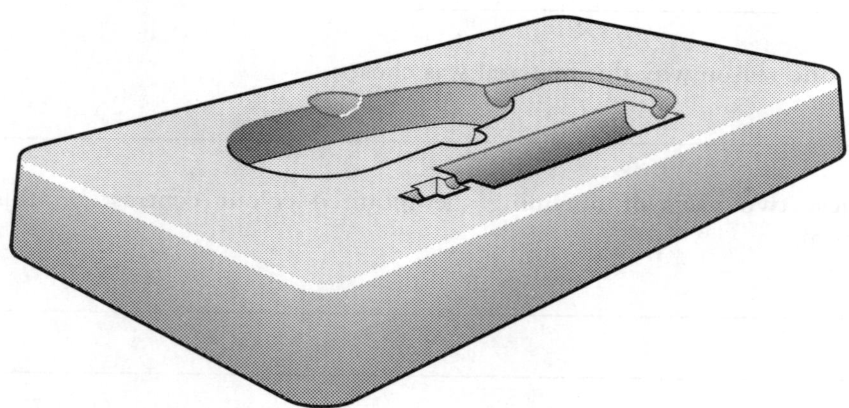

(*a*) Add **three** further requirements to the list below for the **pattern** to be used to vacuum form the package.

1. The pattern should be made from solid material.
2. It should be the correct size.
3. __________ 1 0
4. __________ 1 0
5. __________ 1 0

(*b*) After forming the package, the plastic partly returns to its original shape after the vacuum is switched off.

Give a reason why this happened.

____

____

____

__________ 2

__________ 1 0

[*END OF QUESTION PAPER*]

SCOTTISH CERTIFICATE OF EDUCATION 1996

MONDAY, 27 MAY
1.15 PM – 2.15 PM

CRAFT AND DESIGN STANDARD GRADE
Credit Level

ATTEMPT ALL QUESTIONS

1. A design for a table, which is to stand against a wall, is shown below.

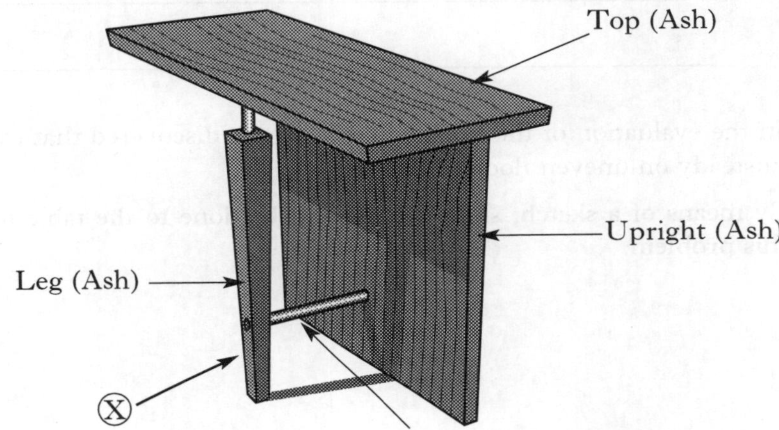

(*a*) The top and the upright are made from solid ash. Suggest **two** methods of joining the top to the upright. (You may wish to use sketches to help explain your answer.)

1 0

1 0

(*b*) The leg is made from solid ash.

(i) Why is it easier to drill hole (X) before the leg is planed to a taper?

____

____ 1 0

(ii) Give **one** reason why a **jack plane** should be used in preference to a smoothing plane for tapering the leg.

____

____ 1 0

(iii) How is the leg held and prevented from moving,

1. when planing the first taper?

____

____ 1 0

2. when planing the last taper?

____

____ 1 0

(c) (i) In the evaluation of the finished table, it was discovered that the table was unsteady on uneven floors.

By means of a sketch, show what could be done to the table to overcome this problem.

1 0

(ii) Why did the designer not put the rail closer to the bottom of the leg, where it might have given more support?

____

____ 1 0

(iii) The upright is **not** close to the back edge of the table top. Suggest **one** reason why it is not positioned closer to the edge.

____

____ 1 0

(d) When the ash was finished with clear varnish, the designer did not like the silver colour of the aluminium against the pale gold of the ash.

Suggest another metal which might give a better match.

____ 1 0

2. A pupil's design for a desk tidy is shown below.

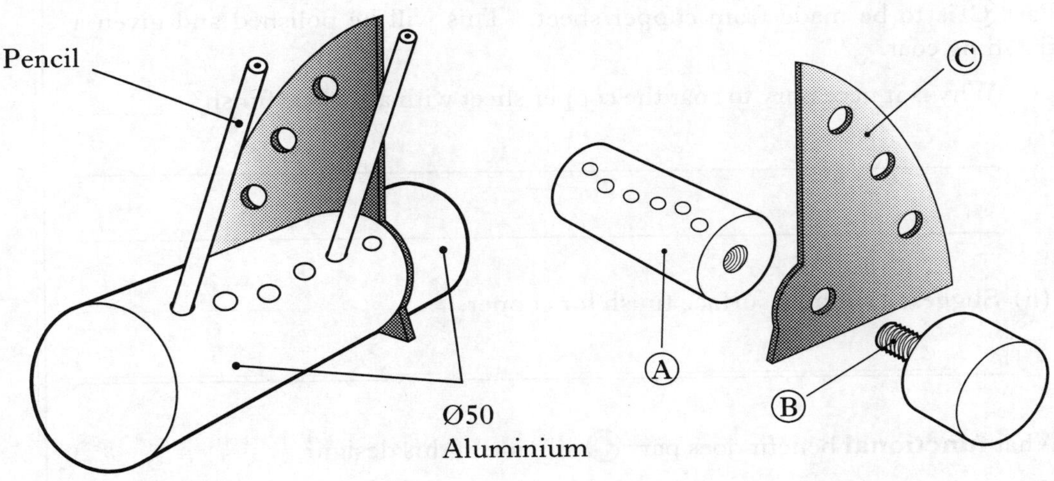

Pencil

Ⓒ

Ⓐ

Ⓑ

Ø50
Aluminium

(*a*) (i) Explain why the thread in part Ⓐ should be cut before the thread in part Ⓑ.

____

____ 1

____ 0

(ii) Name **two** of the taps that should be used to cut a full thread in part Ⓐ. 1

____________________ tap 0

1

____________________ tap 0

(*b*) The holes for the pencils in part Ⓐ were drilled on a pillar drill. Describe how part Ⓐ should have been held while it was being drilled.

____

____ 2

1

____ 0

(*c*) Part Ⓒ is to be made from copper sheet. This will be polished and given a finishing coat.

(i) Why is it necessary to coat the copper sheet with a surface finish?

____

____ 1 0

(ii) Suggest a suitable surface finish for copper.

____ 1 0

(*d*) What **functional** benefit does part Ⓒ provide in this design?

____

____ 1 0

3. The frame for the racing bicycle below is made from a new lightweight plastic.

The Velo
Designed by
Michael Conrad and Dieter Raefler

Write down **three** other properties that this plastic should have to make it suitable for use in this design.

1. ____ 1 0

2. ____ 1 0

3. ____ 1 0

4. The aluminium handle shown below has been made on a metalwork lathe.

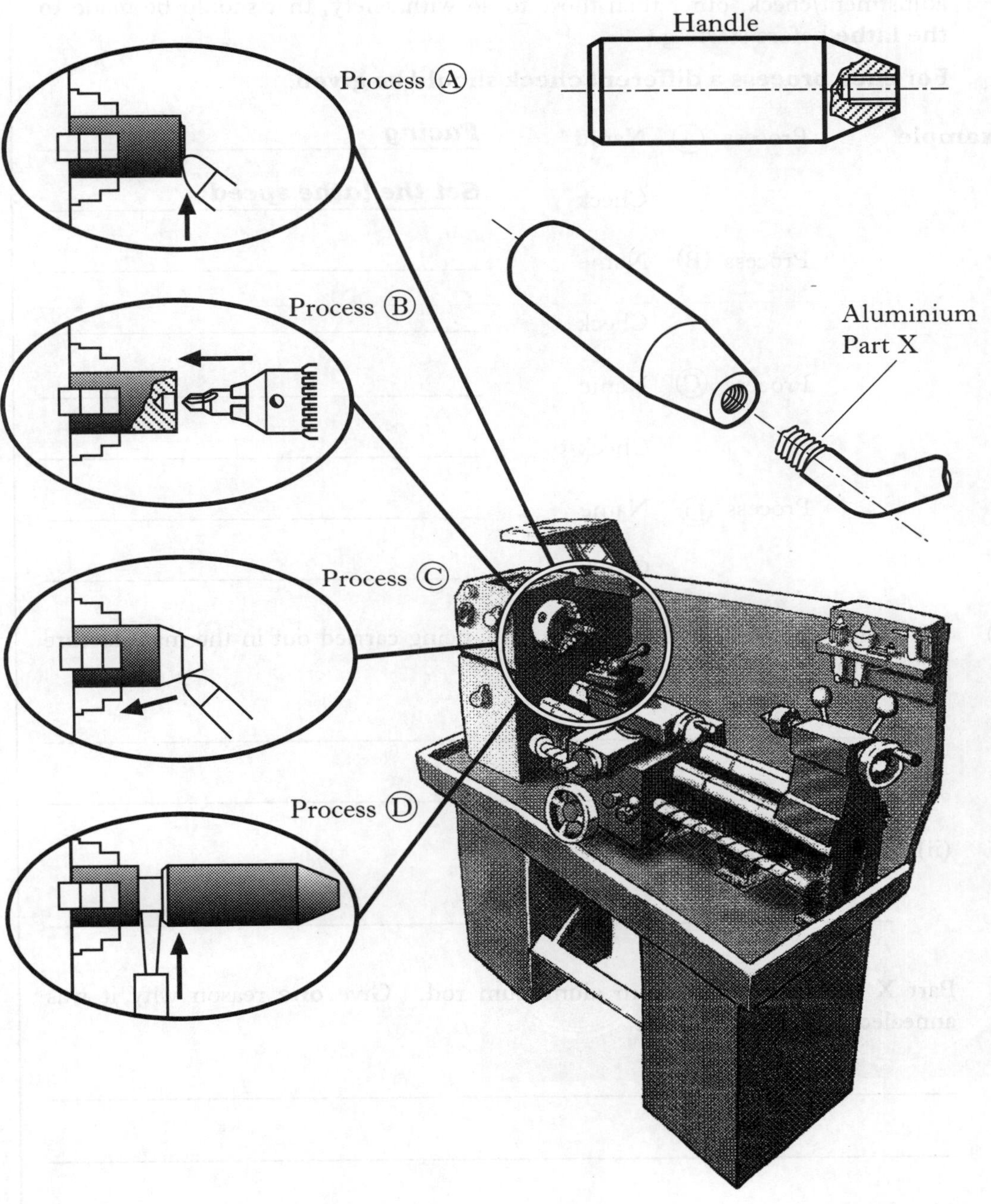

Diagrams of some of the stages in the manufacture of the handle have been shown alongside the lathe.

(*a*) For each stage, name the turning process being carried out and describe **one** adjustment/check, other than those to do with safety, that should be made **to the lathe** before starting.

For each process a different check should be given.

Example Process (A) Name ***Facing***

Check ***Set the lathe speed***

Process (B) Name ________________ 1 0

Check ________________ 1 0

Process (C) Name ________________ 1 0

Check ________________ 1 0

Process (D) Name ________________ 1 0

Check ________________ 1 0

(*b*) (i) Give **one** reason why process (B) is being carried out in the manufacture of the handle.

____

________________________________ 1 0

(ii) Name the tool used in process (B).

________________________________ 1 0

(*c*) Part X has been made from aluminium rod. Give **one** reason why it was annealed before it was bent.

____

________________________________ 1 0

5. A scale model of a pupil's design for a desk is shown below.

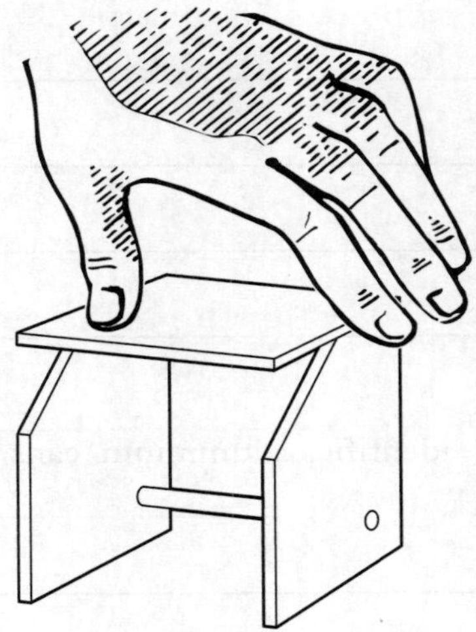

(*a*) Name **one** material that could be used to make the model. Give **two** properties of the material that make it suitable for this model.

Name of material ________________ 1 0

Property 1. ________________

________________ 1 0

Property 2. ________________

________________ 1 0

(*b*) Give **two** reasons why the scale of the model should be carefully chosen.

1. ________________

________________ 1 0

2. ________________

________________ 1 0

(*c*) Write down **one** piece of information that cannot be found out from this scale model of the desk.

____

________________ 1 0

6. (*a*) (i) How does the world's environment benefit when people put used aluminium cans into a recycling bank?

____

____

____

____

2
1
0

(ii) Give a simple test that identifies aluminium cans from other metal cans.

____

____

1
0

(*b*) (i) How does the world's environment benefit when people use MDF and chipboard instead of solid wood?

____

____

____

____

2
1
0

(ii) Which of these materials (MDF, chipboard or solid wood) is most suitable for a painted finish?

____

____

1
0

7. An extract from the development work in a pupil's folio is shown below.

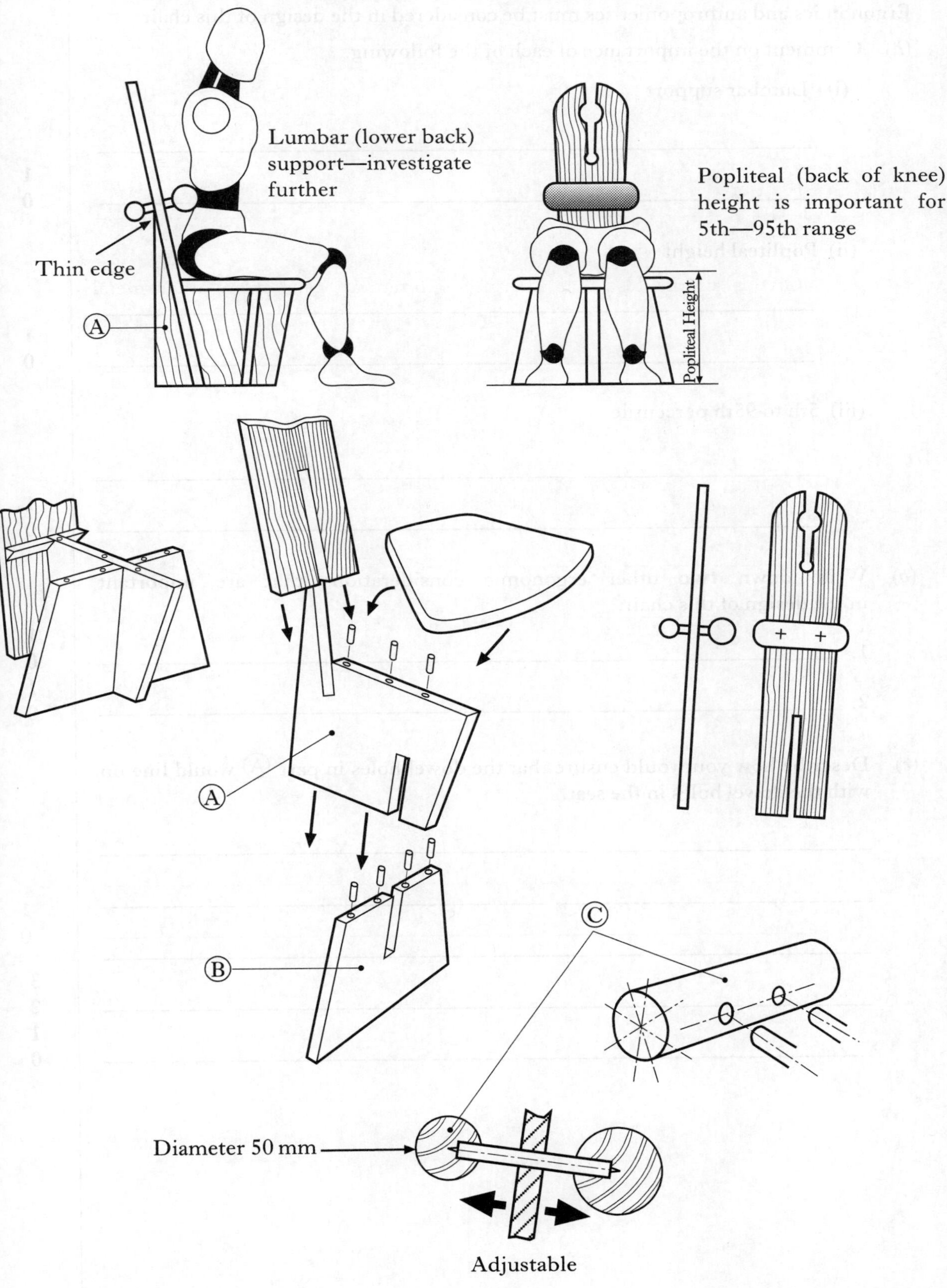

Ergonomics and anthropometrics must be considered in the design of this chair.

(*a*) Comment on the importance of each of the following.

(i) Lumbar support

____

______________________________ 1 0

(ii) Popliteal height

____

______________________________ 1 0

(iii) 5th to 95th percentile

____

______________________________ 1 0

(*b*) Write down **two** other ergonomic considerations that are important in the design of this chair.

1. ______________________________ 1 0

2. ______________________________ 1 0

(*c*) Describe how you would ensure that the dowel holes in part Ⓐ would line up with the dowel holes in the seat.

____

____

____

____

______________________________ 3 2 1 0

(*d*) It is not good wood working practice to have such a thin edge on part Ⓐ. Show on a sketch how this could be improved.

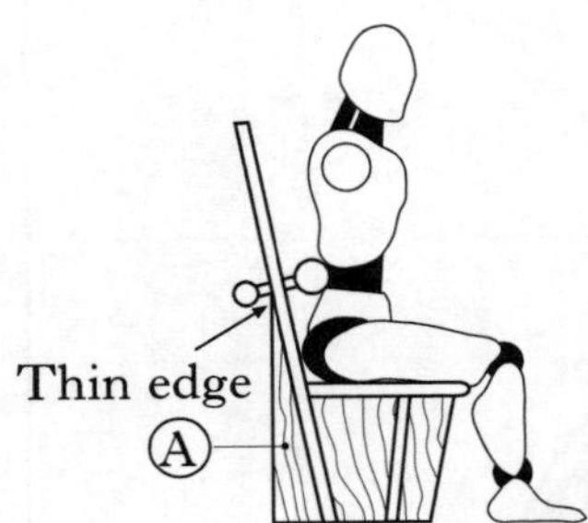

2
1
0

(*e*) Part Ⓒ has been turned on a wood lathe between centres.

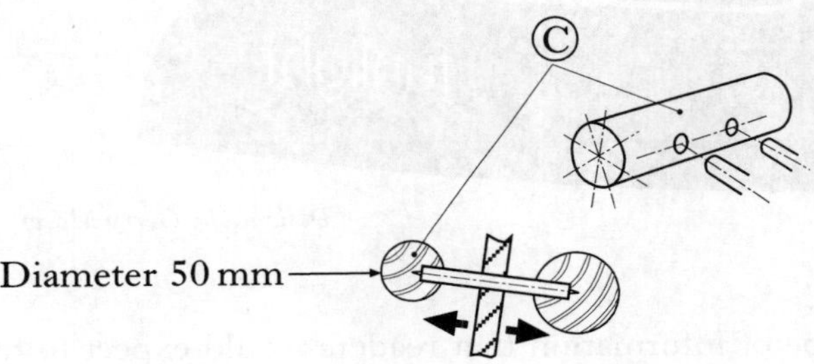

(i) Give **one** reason why a saw cut was made on one end of the wood before it was mounted on the lathe.

____

____ 1 0

(ii) A revolving centre was used in the tailstock to support the other end of the wood. What advantage has a revolving centre over a dead centre?

____

____ 1 0

(iii) How could the diameter of part Ⓒ be measured accurately?

____

____ 1 0

8. A consumer report comparing the hand held flashlight shown below with more traditional torches has been published.

Designed by Gerry Meyer

Give **three** examples of the type of information that readers would expect to find in the report to help them to make comparisons.

1. ____

____ **1 0**

2. ____

____ **1 0**

3. ____

____ **1 0**

9. How could the Health and Safety of others be affected if you

(i) left sharp-edged tools on top of a workshop bench when you had finished using them?

____

____ **1 0**

(ii) used spray paint in an area without suitable ventilation?

____

____ **1 0**

(iii) stored a liquid such as thinners or white spirit in an old lemonade bottle?

____

____ **1 0**

(iv) failed to report a breakage or fault in workshop equipment or machinery?

____

____ **1 0**

[*END OF QUESTION PAPER*]

SCOTTISH
CERTIFICATE OF
EDUCATION
1997

MONDAY, 26 MAY
1.00 PM – 2.00 PM

CRAFT AND DESIGN
STANDARD GRADE
Credit Level

1 Answer all the questions.

2 Read every question carefully before you answer.

3 Write your answers in the spaces provided.

4 Do **not** write in the margins.

5 All dimensions are given in millimetres.

6 Before leaving the examination room you must give this book to the invigilator. If you do not, you may lose all the marks for this paper.

ATTEMPT ALL QUESTIONS

1. A designer has been asked to produce a number of ideas for items in a children's playground, and to present them in the form of prototypes.

(*a*) (i) Suggest a user group or organisation which the designer could consult to research this brief.

1
0

(ii) What is meant by the term **prototype**?

1
0

(*b*) State one reason why the designer might want to use a **scale model**.

1
0

(*c*) When **evaluating** a product, to which other stage of the **design process** should you refer?

1
0

2.

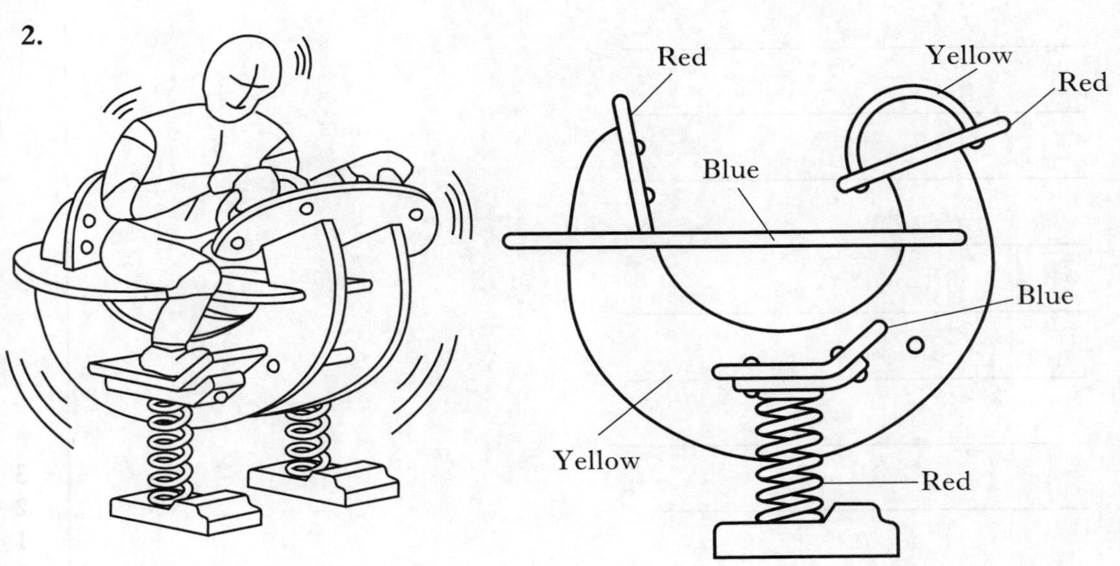

The sketch above shows the final design of one piece of playground equipment, a bouncer.

(*a*) Three items on the specification for the bouncer are listed below. Suggest another **two**.

- It must be safe.
- It must be finished in primary colours.
- The costs must fall within the customer budget.
- ____
- ____

2 1 0

(*b*) Suggest one reason why the specification has asked for primary colours to be used on this product.

____

1 0

(*c*) Unfortunately the coil springs will corrode if exposed to the weather. They are to be protected by **plastic dip-coating**. Suggest **one** further reason for choosing this process to give an appropriate finish.

____

1 0

(*d*) Describe the dip-coating process. Sketches may be used to illustrate your answer.

____

____

____

____

____

____

____

____

____

____

3 2 1 0

3.

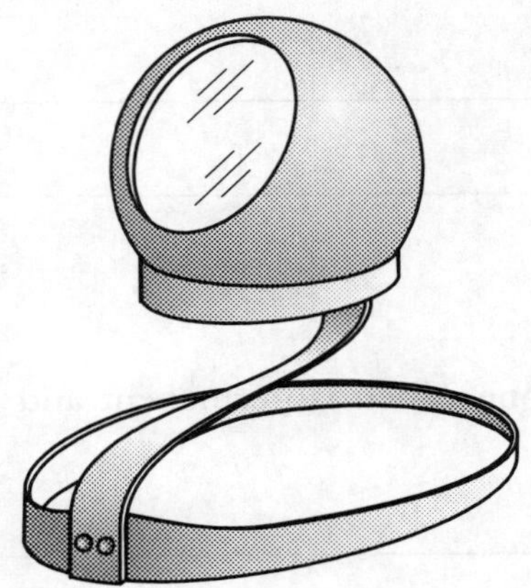

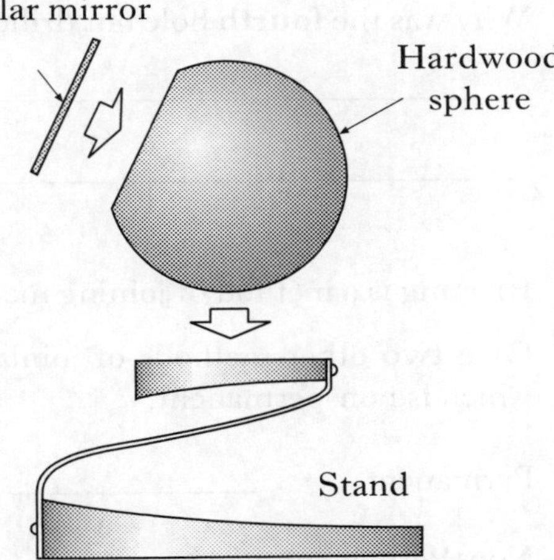

A base-stand had to be designed for a spherical "eyeball" mirror. It was decided that a metal stand would be appropriate.

(*a*) What **functional** advantage can be gained because the sphere is free to move in the stand?

____

____ **1**
0

(*b*) It was decided to use **flat-head rivets** to join the stem to the hoops.

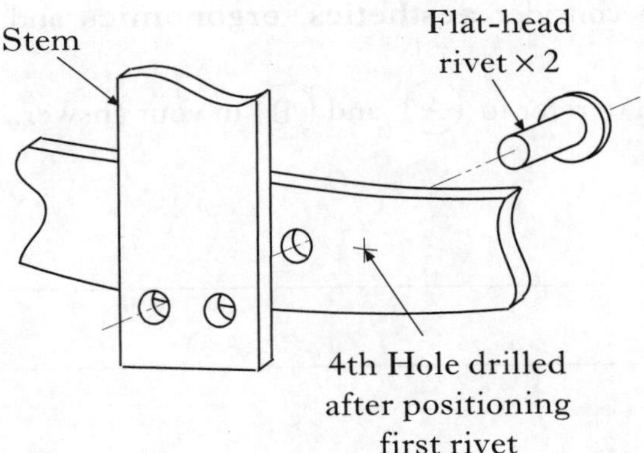

Name the tool required to **form** the snap-head of the rivet as illustrated above.

____ **1**
0

(*c*) Three holes have been shown in the sketch on the left.

Why was the **fourth** hole not drilled?

____

____ 1 0

(*d*) Riveting is a method of joining metals.

Give **two** other methods of joining metals, one which is permanent and one which is non-permanent.

Permanent ______________________________ 2

Non-Permanent ______________________________ 1 0

4.

The illustration shows two different types of computer mouse.

Type (A) was designed and manufactured in the 1980s, and type (B) was designed and manufactured in the 1990s.

The designers of both products had to consider **aesthetics**, **ergonomics** and **anthropometrics**.

Explain these **three** terms. You may wish to refer to (A) and (B) in your answer.

Ergonomics

____

____ 1 0

Anthropometrics

____

____ 1 0

Aesthetics

____

____ 1 0

5.

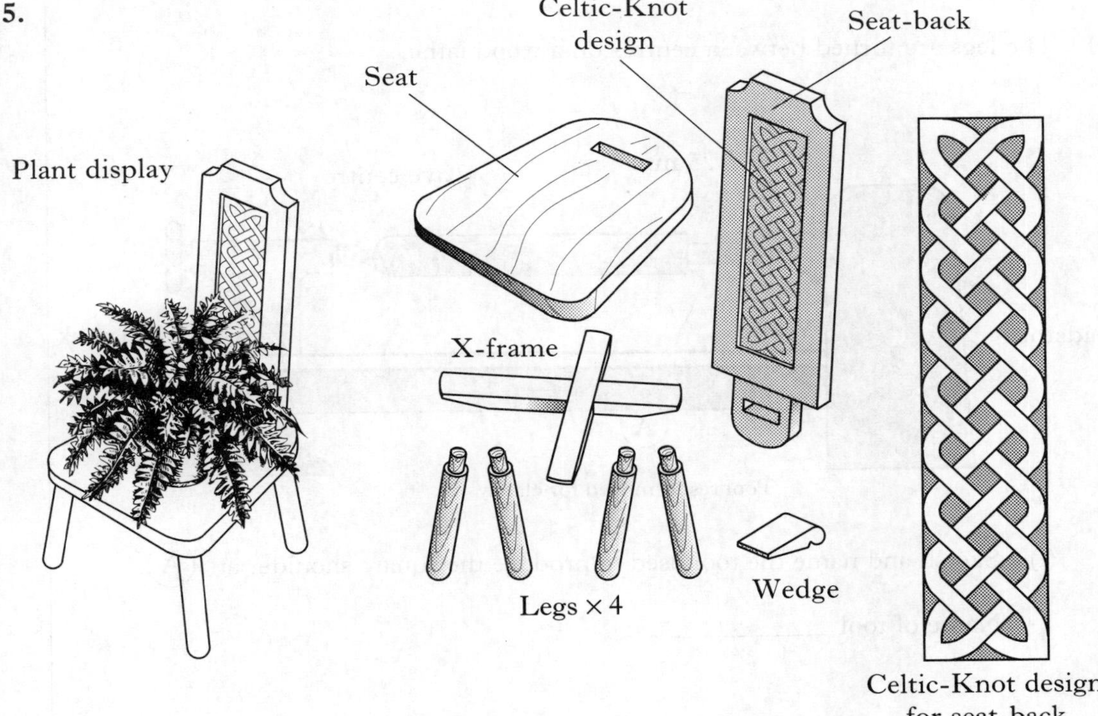

FLAT-PACK COMPONENTS

A design for a traditional style of spinning-stool has been adapted for mass-production. A **Celtic-Knot** design is to be cut into the chairback by means of an automatic-machining operation, ie CAD/CAM.

(*a*) This item comes flat-packed for self-assembly. Explain these terms.

Self-assembly ______________________________

______________________________ 1 0

Flat-packed ______________________________

______________________________ 1 0

(*b*) A polythene sheet is used when shrinkwrapping all the loose components together prior to the final packing of the product in protective cardboard packaging.

Polythene is a **thermoplastic**. Explain what is meant by "thermoplastic".

______________________________ 1 0

Name another example of a thermoplastic.

______________________________ 1 0

(*c*) The legs are turned between centres on a wood lathe.

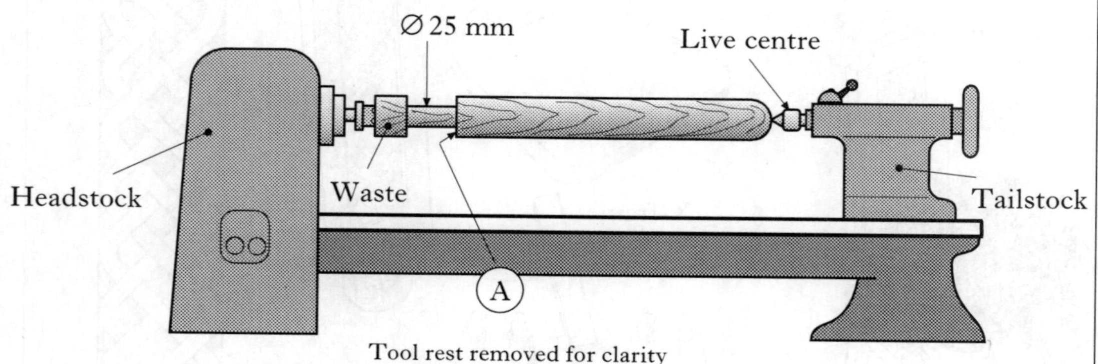

Tool rest removed for clarity

(i) Sketch and name the tool used to produce the square shoulder at (A).

Name of tool ______________

1 0 1 0

(ii) Sketch and name the tool used to check the Ø 25 near (A).

Name of tool ______________

1 0 1 0

6.

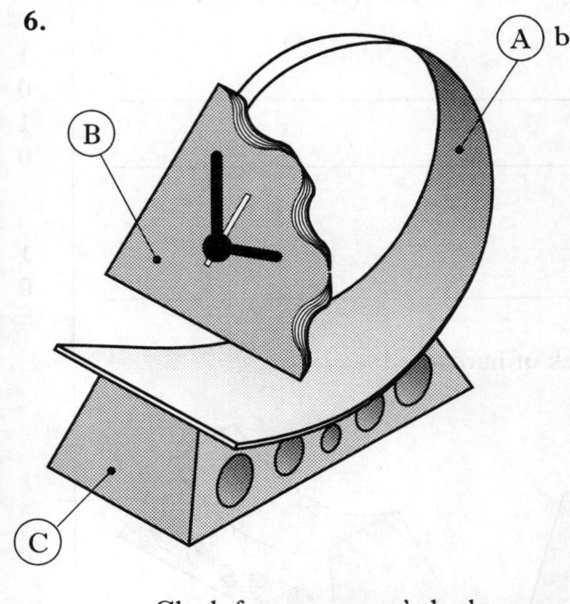

Clock for a teenager's bedroom

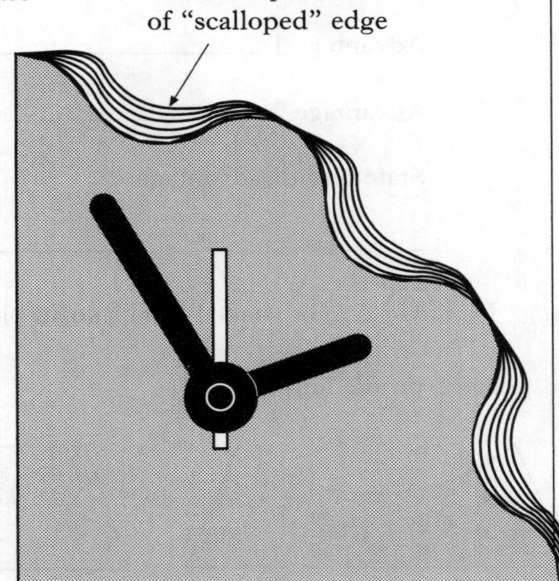

(*a*) When forming part (A), the brass sheet will become **work hardened**. In order to make it **malleable**, it will have to be **annealed**.

Explain these terms.

Work hardened ______________________ 1 0

Malleable ______________________ 1 0

Annealed ______________________ 1 0

(*b*) Part (B) is to be constructed from 12 mm birch plywood. The clockface is to be coloured with a blue **water-based** wood dye.

(i) List the stages of preparation necessary to provide the **best possible surface finish** prior to the dye being applied to the clock face.

____

____

______________________ 3 2 1 0

(ii) Which **hand-tool** could be used to shape and form the **scalloped edge** to expose the different layers of the plywood to provide a contrast to the geometric shape?

______________________ 1 0

(iii) State **two** advantages of using plywood for part (B) in preference to natural timber.

Advantage 1 ______________________________ 1 0

Advantage 2 ______________________________ 1 0

State **one** disadvantage.

______________________________ 1 0

(*c*) Part (C) is to be shaped from a **solid** block of hardwood.

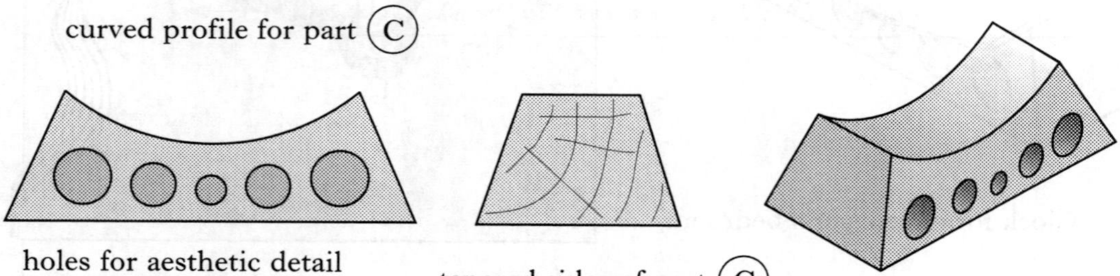

curved profile for part (C)

holes for aesthetic detail – ∅25, ∅15 and ∅10 mm

tapered sides of part (C)

Why would it be preferable to remove the curved profile and drill the holes **before** tapering the sides?

____

______________________________ 1 0

(*d*) Which type of drill-bit would produce clean, flat bottomed holes in part (C)?

______________________________ 1 0

(*e*) Suggest a suitable finish for each of the parts (A), (B) and (C).

(A) Polished brass ______________________________ 1 0

(B) Water-dyed birch plywood ______________________________ 1 0

(C) Hardwood ______________________________ 1 0

7. Brass is an alloy of **copper and zinc**.

(*a*) Name one other **alloy**.

______________________________ 1 0

(*b*) Explain why metals are **alloyed**.

______________________________ 1 0

8.

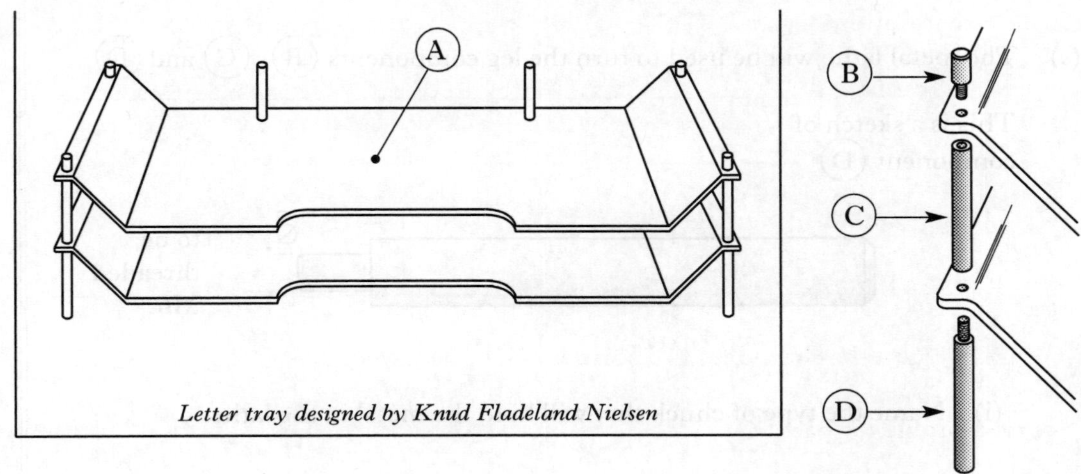

Letter tray designed by Knud Fladeland Nielsen

Construction details for leg components

The letter tray illustrated above is constructed from brass rod and acrylic sheet. It is intended for use in an office or at a workstation.

(*a*) What is the **functional** reason for the cut-out on (A)?

________________________________ 1 0

(*b*) Which hand tool could be used to make the cut-out from the acrylic sheet prior to bending?

________________________________ 1 0

(*c*) Identify **two methods** of preventing the acrylic sheet from **cracking or chipping** when drilling out the clearance holes for the legs.

Method 1 ________________________ 2 1

Method 2 ________________________ 0

(*d*) List **two** advantages of using a mould for forming the acrylic trays.

____

________________________________ 2 1

________________________________ 0

(*e*) The metal lathe will be used to turn the leg components (B), (C) and (D) .

This is a sketch of component (D)

Ø6

to be threaded M6

(i) Name the type of chuck that will hold the metal in the lathe.

______________________________ 1 0

(ii) Write down the sequence of turning operations required to produce part (D) .

1. Face off both ends.

2. ______________________________

3. ______________________________ 3 2 1

4. ______________________________ 0

(iii) Name the **tool** that should be used to give an accurate check that the diameter (Ø) of the part to be threaded is 6 mm.

______________________________ 1 0

(iv) What is the purpose of the **chamfer** on the part to be threaded?

______________________________ 1 0

(*f*) Name the hand tool which will be used to cut an **external** thread on part (D).

1
0

____

(*g*) When preparing to cut the **external** thread, which **adjustment screw** should be tightened first?

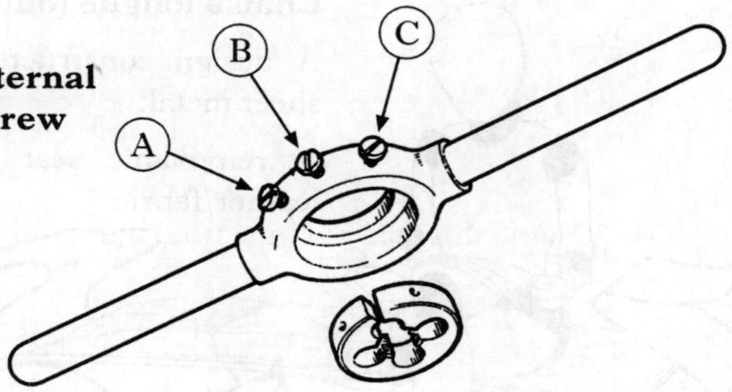

A
B
C

____

1
0

(*h*) (i) Circle the correct **tapping size hole** for an **M6** thread on the list given below.

The tapping drill size is **∅6·0** **∅5·0** **∅5·5** **∅6·5**.

1
0

(ii) Name the tap you should use **first** when threading.

____

1
0

[*END OF QUESTION PAPER*]

SCOTTISH CERTIFICATE OF EDUCATION 1998

MONDAY, 25 MAY 10.30 AM – 11.30 AM

CRAFT AND DESIGN STANDARD GRADE
Credit Level

ATTEMPT ALL QUESTIONS

1.

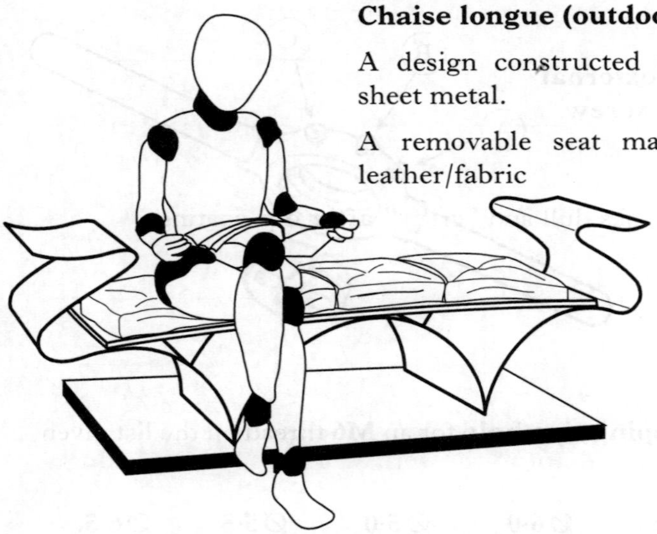

Piers Gough
Chaise longue (outdoor bench)

A design constructed from folded and welded sheet metal.

A removable seat mattress is upholstered in leather/fabric

(*a*) Identify **one** ergonomic factor which may have influenced the design of this chaise longue.

________________________________ 1 0

(*b*) Suggest **two** anthropometric considerations with regards to the design of the seat.

(i) ________________________________ 1 0

(ii) ________________________________ 1 0

(*c*) Comment on **two** aspects of the aesthetic appeal of this design.

(i) ________________________________ 1 0

(ii) ________________________________ 1 0

(*d*) Name **two** types of coloured finish that could be applied to the unprotected steel.

(i) ________________________________ 1 0

(ii) ________________________________ 1 0

2. The finish applied to a pupil's project may show signs of poor preparation and application.

For each case given below, state the most likely cause of the obvious fault in the applied finish.

(*a*) There are varnish **runs** visible on a finished wooden surface.

1
0

(*b*) On metal, the plastic coating looks dull and "gritty" **after** dip-coating.

1
0

(*c*) A coat of gloss paint has "**soaked into**" the surface of a piece of medium density fibreboard.

1
0

(*d*) Scratches can be seen on the **polished** edges of a finished piece of acrylic.

1
0

(*e*) When dry, a varnished finish feels very "**gritty**" to the touch.

1
0

3. A pupil's initial designs for a candle holder are shown.

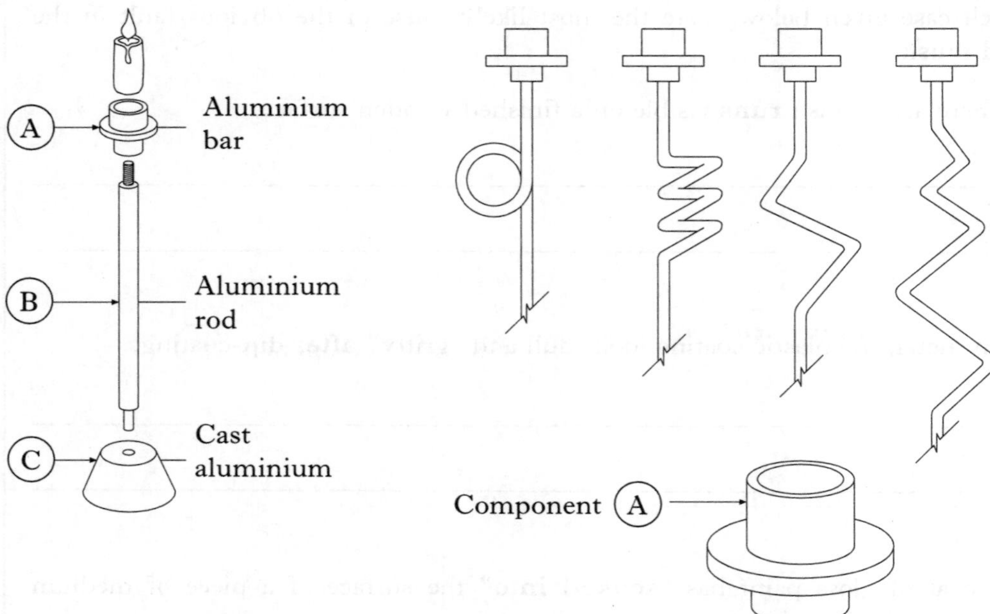

(*a*) (i) What is the function of the shoulder on component (A)?

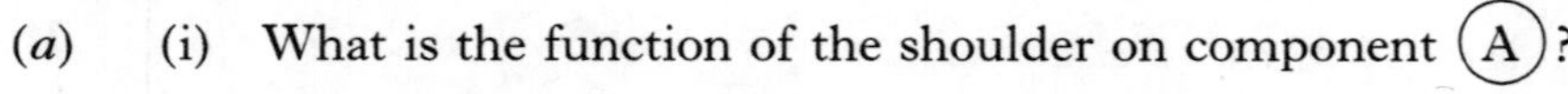

1
0

(ii) Name **one** other non-ferrous metal that would be suitable for component (A).

1
0

(*b*) (i) To achieve some of the different shapes shown in the sketches, the aluminium rod must first be annealed. Why is this process necessary?

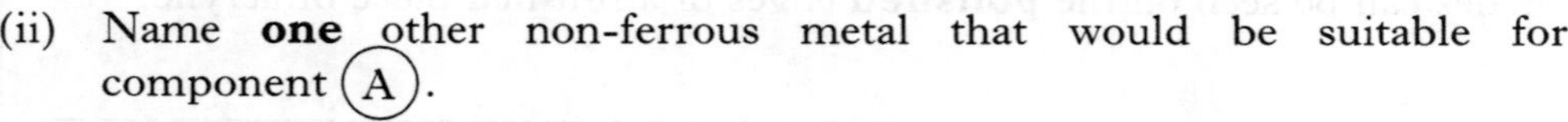

1
0

(ii) When annealing, suggest a method of testing the correct temperature of the aluminium.

1
0

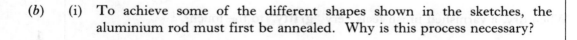

(*c*) In order to cast the aluminium base, a wooden pattern is produced. Why is a good quality finish required on the pattern?

1
0

(*d*) List in sequence three further stages required to produce the **internal** thread in component (C).

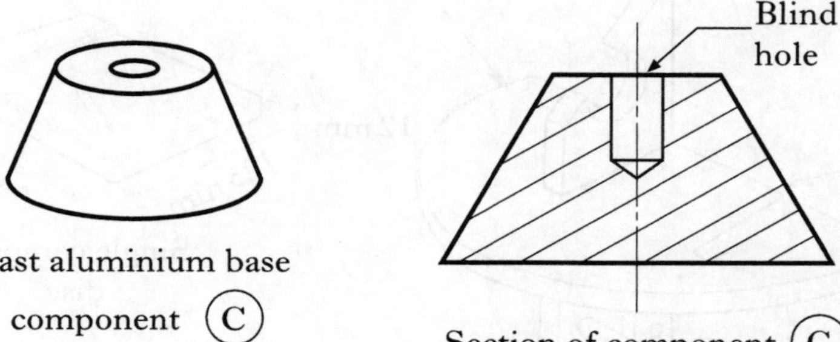

Cast aluminium base component (C)

Section of component (C)

Stage (i) Use a centre punch to mark the position of the blind hole.

Stage (ii) ______________________________

Stage (iii) ______________________________

Stage (iv) ______________________________

3 2 1 0

(*e*) The aluminium rod is to be threaded at each end.

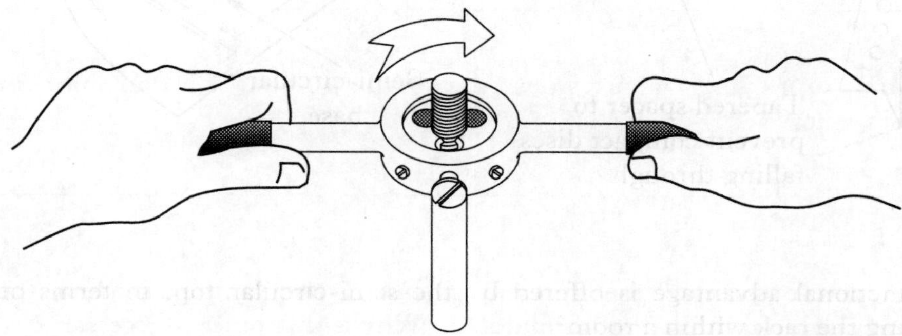

The initial thread was cut and found to be **too tight** a fit.

Describe how to adjust the split-circular die so that the thread is an "**easy running fit**".

____

____

____

____

2 1 0

4. A pupil's design for a free-standing CD rack is illustrated below.

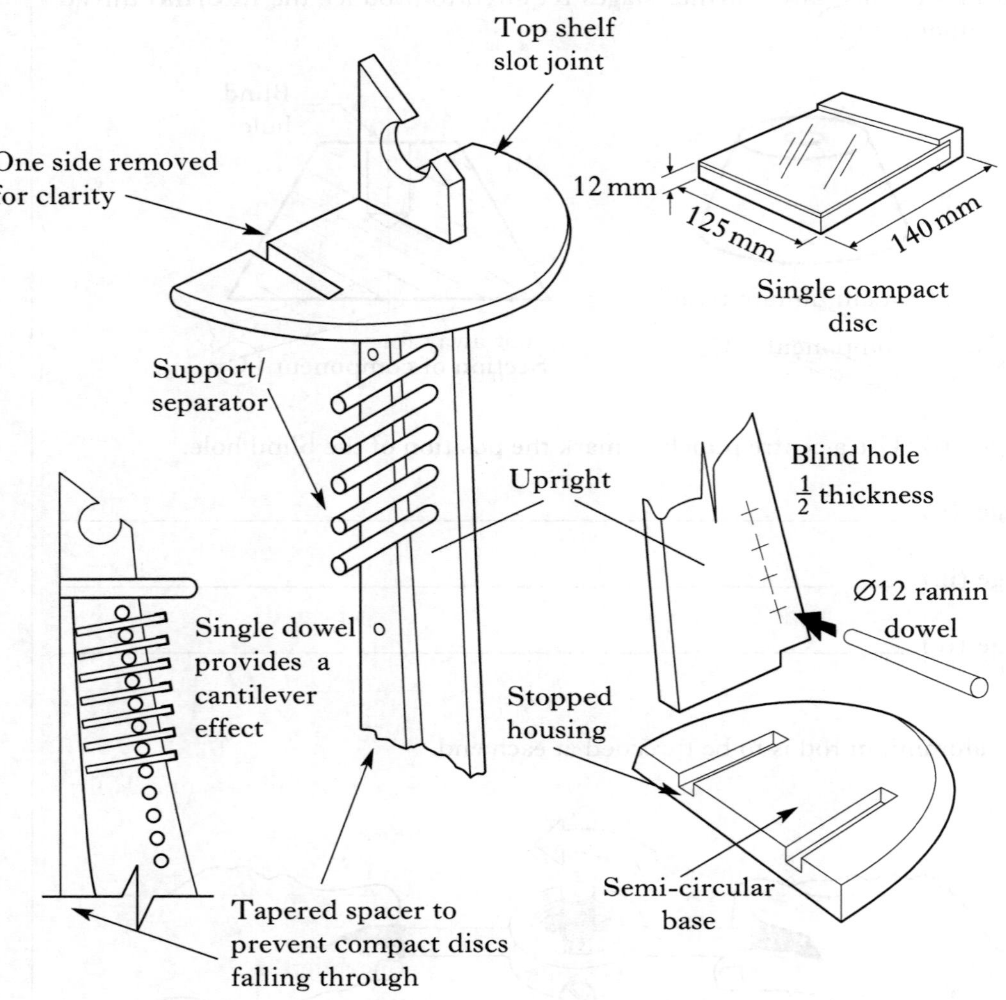

(*a*) What functional advantage is offered by the semi-circular top, in terms of positioning the rack within a room?

____ **1 0**

(*b*) Comment on the following aspects of this design.

(i) Function ____________________________ **1 0**

(ii) Ergonomics ____________________________ **1 0**

(iii) Aesthetics ____________________________ **1 0**

(iv) Construction ____________________________ **1 0**

(*c*) The uprights of the rack are secured to the base using stopped housing joints as illustrated.

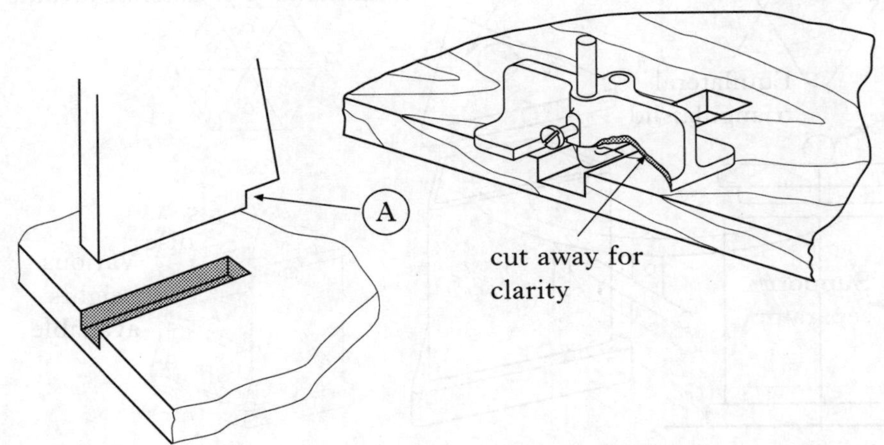

(i) What is the benefit of removing the notch (A) indicated?

____ **1** **0**

(ii) Why would a hand-router, rather than a chisel, be more suitable for "finishing" the bottom of the housing joint?

____ **1** **0**

(iii) Explain how you would set this tool to the required depth.

____

____ **1** **0**

5.

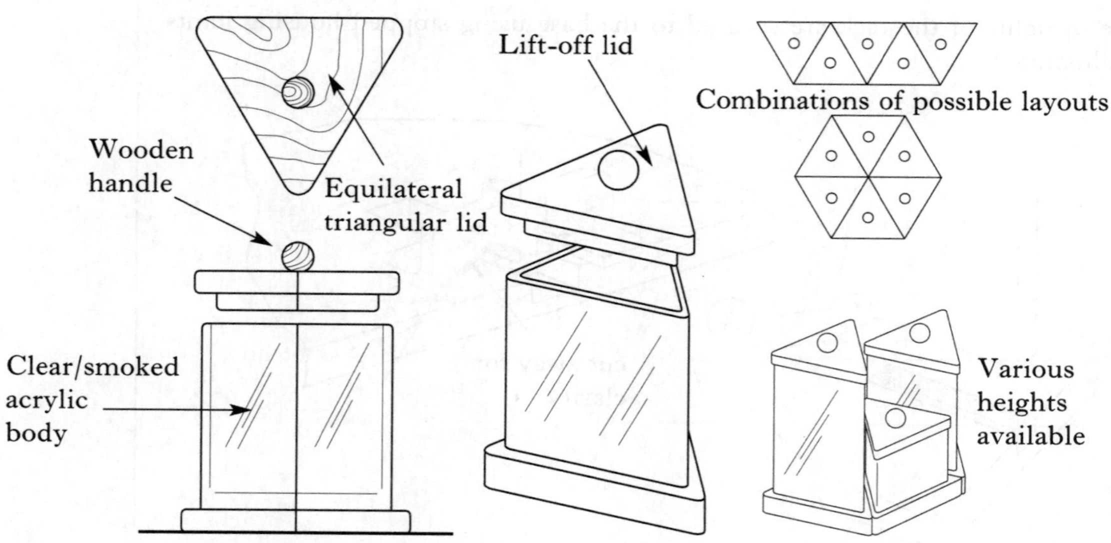

The initial sketches shown above are ideas for a range of modular kitchen storage containers. These are made from acrylic and wood, and used to store such items as pasta, rice and dried goods. Several of these containers are required to make a set.

(*a*) With regards to storage and display, state **one** advantage and **one** disadvantage of the triangular prism design.

Advantage ________________________________ 1 0

Disadvantage ________________________________ 1 0

(b) (i) Suggest how you might accurately locate the centre of the equilateral triangle before drilling.

Use this sketch as part of your answer.

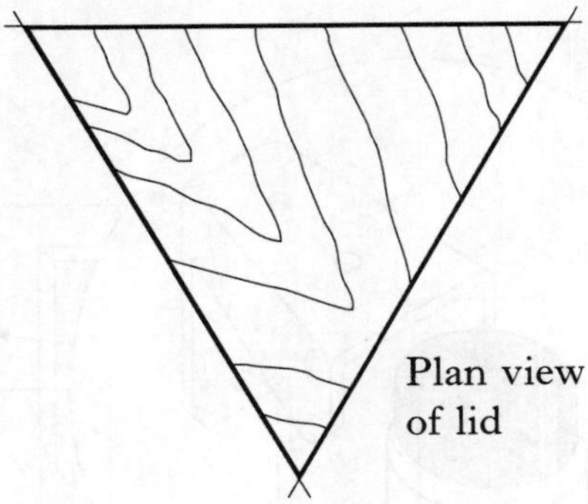

Plan view of lid

1
0

(ii) Complete the following diagram to show the holes required for fixing the handle to the lid.
On the diagram, label the following: a pilot hole; a clearance hole; and a countersink hole.

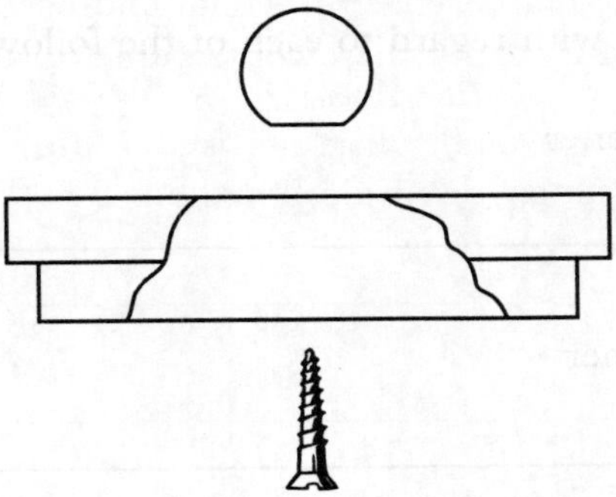

3
2
1
0

(c) When manufacturing the prototype, the forming of the acrylic tube was produced **without** the aid of a former/jig.

(i) If a **former/jig** were to be used, why would this be an advantage for batch-production?

1
0

(ii) With regard to marking out for batch-production, how would you ensure that the wooden triangles for the lids are the correct size and shape?

1
0

6. A design for a jar opener is shown below.
The opener can be mounted on a wall or under a cabinet.

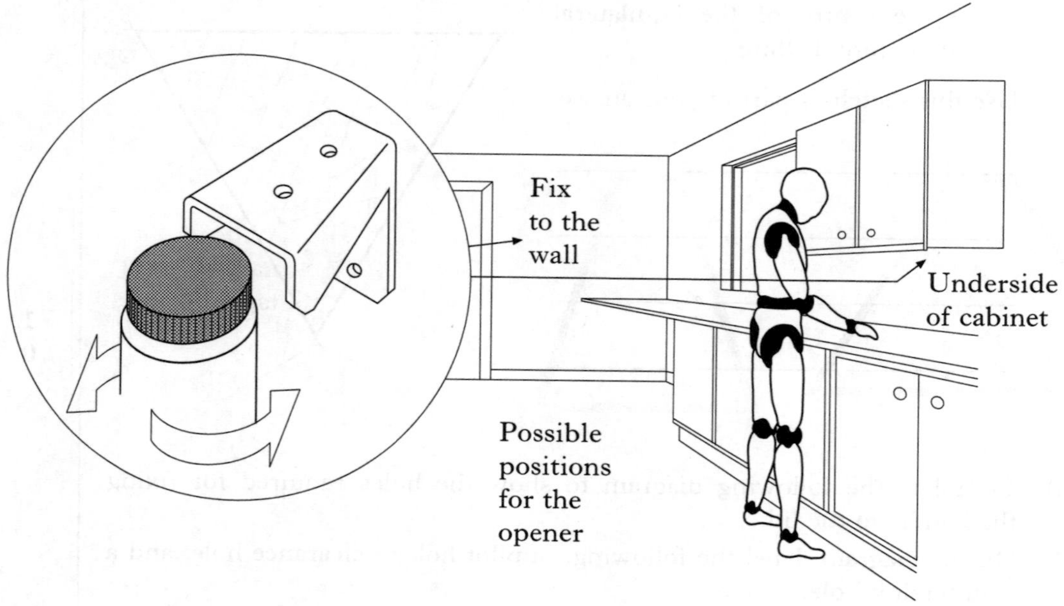

(a) List **one** consideration with regard to each of the following.

(i) Access to the opener

______________________________ 1 0

(ii) Users of the opener

______________________________ 1 0

(iii) Fixing of the opener

______________________________ 1 0

(iv) Safety

______________________________ 1 0

(*b*) As part of the research to determine the best angle of the taper for the opener, it was necessary to investigate various sizes of lids for jars.

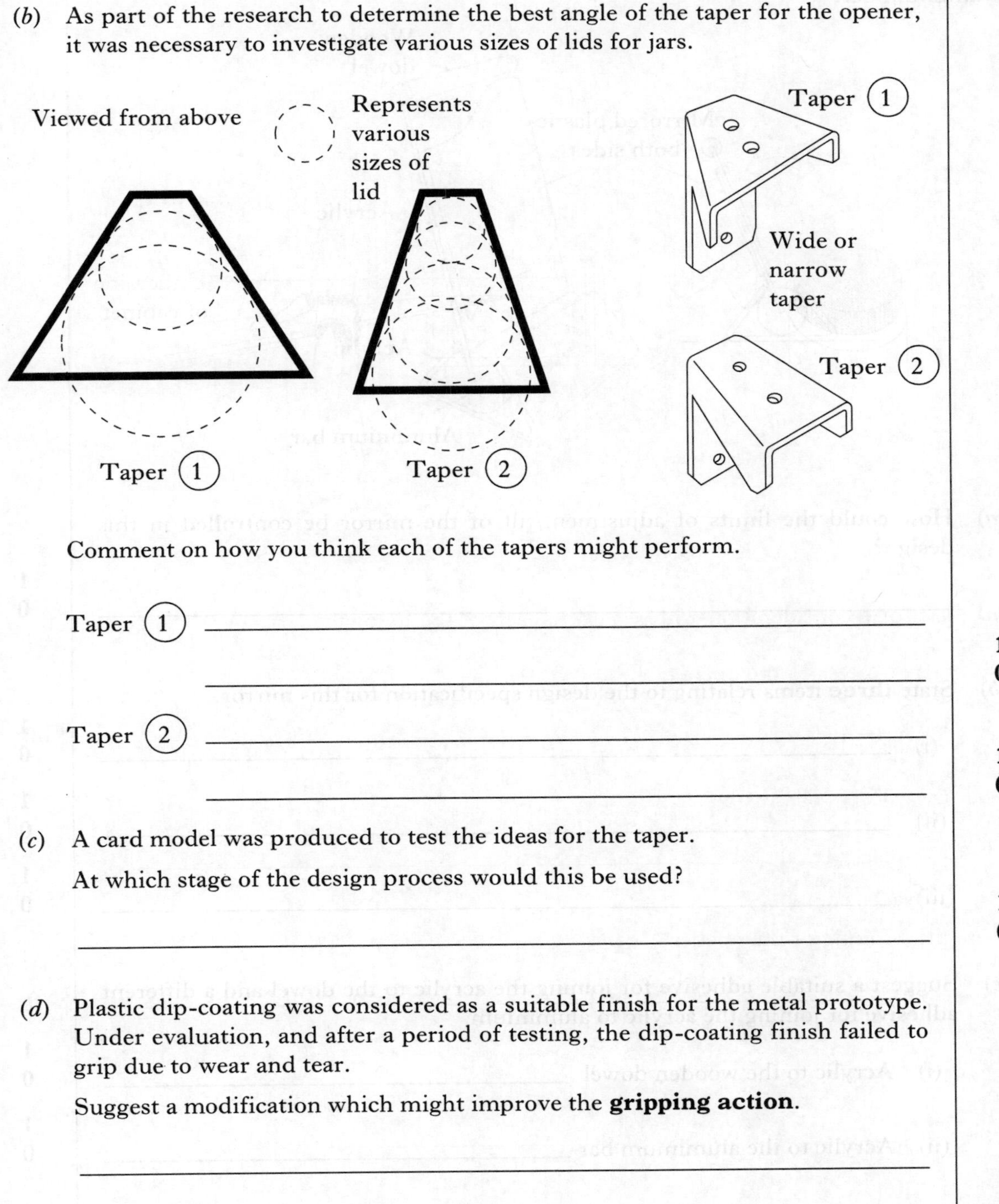

Comment on how you think each of the tapers might perform.

Taper 1 ______________________________

______________________________ 1 0

Taper 2 ______________________________

______________________________ 1 0

(*c*) A card model was produced to test the ideas for the taper.

At which stage of the design process would this be used?

______________________________ 1 0

(*d*) Plastic dip-coating was considered as a suitable finish for the metal prototype. Under evaluation, and after a period of testing, the dip-coating finish failed to grip due to wear and tear.

Suggest a modification which might improve the **gripping action**.

____

______________________________ 1 0

7. A small adjustable mirror is shown. It is constructed mainly from acrylic and an aluminium bar.

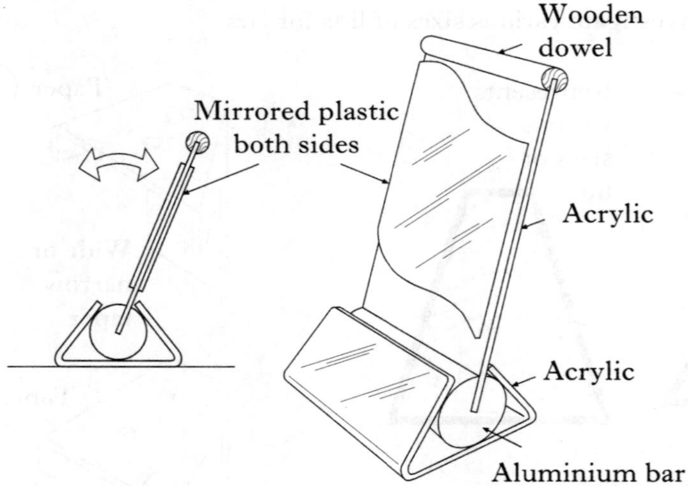

(a) How could the limits of adjustment/tilt of the mirror be controlled in this design?

____ 1 0

(b) State **three** items relating to the design specification for this mirror.

(i) ____ 1 0

(ii) ____ 1 0

(iii) ____ 1 0

(c) Suggest a suitable adhesive for joining the acrylic to the dowel and a different adhesive for joining the acrylic to aluminium.

(i) Acrylic to the wooden dowel ______________________ 1 0

(ii) Acrylic to the aluminium bar ______________________ 1 0 (*d*) When facing off the end of the aluminium bar on the metal lathe, a "**pip**" of material remained on the surface at the centre of the bar.

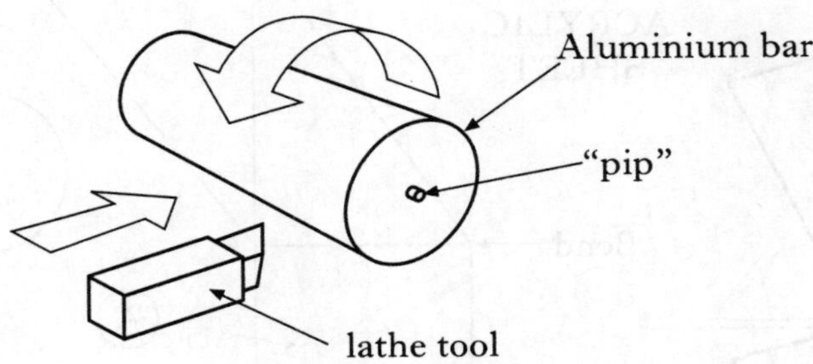

(i) What has caused this to happen?

______________________________________ 1 0

(ii) How should the lathe tool be adjusted to remedy this fault?

______________________________________ 1 0

(iii) State **one** check that could be carried out before the machine is switched on which would have avoided this problem.

______________________________________ 1 0

8. A pupil's design for a desktop clock is shown.

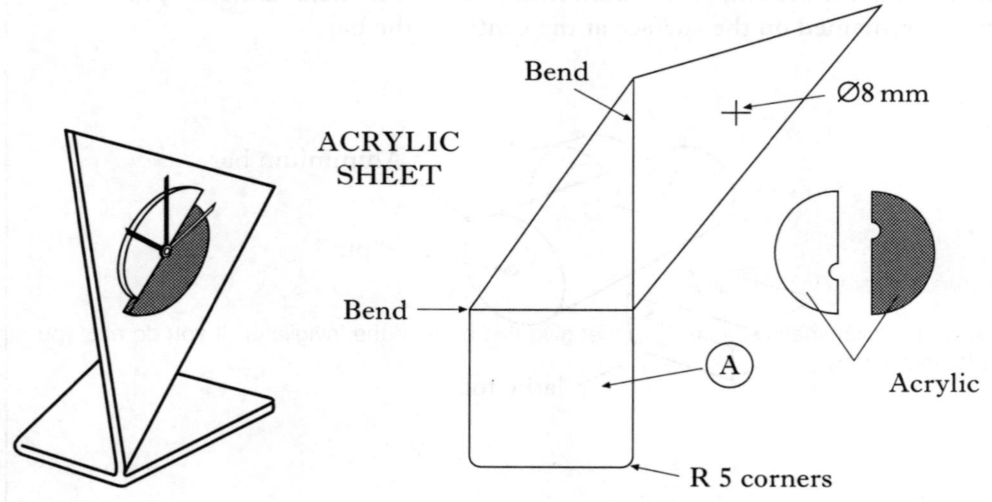

(*a*) State **two** advantages of using acrylic in this construction.

(i) ____________________ 1 0

(ii) ____________________ 1 0

(*b*) Add **two** further parts to the specification.

- The clock must be free-standing.
- ____________________ 2
- ____________________ 1 0

(*c*) Why is it necessary to polish the edges of the acrylic **before** it is formed?

____________________ 1 0

[*END OF QUESTION PAPER*]

SCOTTISH CERTIFICATE OF EDUCATION 1999

TUESDAY, 25 MAY
10.40 AM – 11.40 AM

CRAFT AND DESIGN
STANDARD GRADE
Credit Level

1 Answer all the questions.

2 Read every question carefully before you answer.

3 Write your answers in the spaces provided.

4 Do **not** write in the margins.

5 All dimensions are given in millimetres.

6 Before leaving the examination room you must give this book to the invigilator. If you do not, you may lose all the marks for this paper.

ATTEMPT ALL QUESTIONS

1. A camera is shown below.

Write down **three** pieces of information you would expect to find in a *consumer report* evaluating such a camera.

1 ______________________________ 1 0

2 ______________________________ 1 0

3 ______________________________ 1 0

2. Two chairs are shown below.

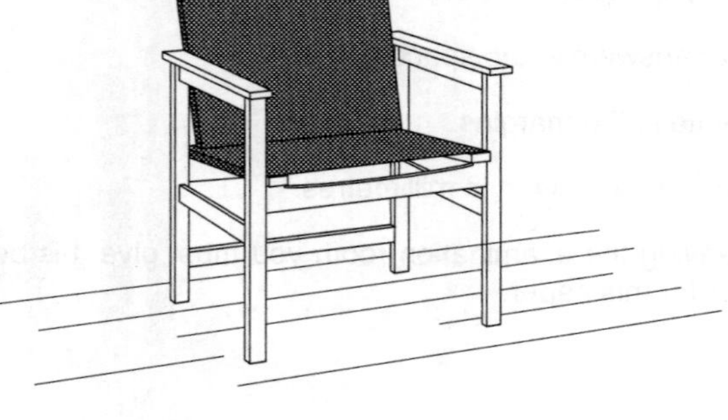

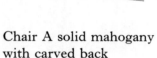

Chair A solid mahogany with carved back

Chair B solid pine with cotton seat and back

(*a*) Why is chair B better for the environment than chair A? 1 0

____

(*b*) Why is chair B easier to mass produce than chair A? 1 0

____

3. A reproduction chair in Mackintosh style is shown. It was made in the school workshop.

(*a*) Part of the chair back is shown below.

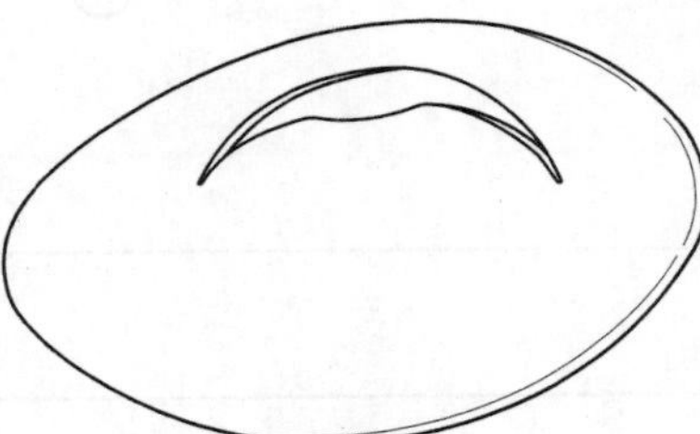

Describe in detail how a drill and coping saw could be used to remove the internal shape. Your answer should include details of how to adjust the coping saw.

____

____

____ 3

____ 2

____ 1

0

(*b*) The tools shown were used during the manufacture of the chair. For **each** tool, describe **two** possible adjustments.

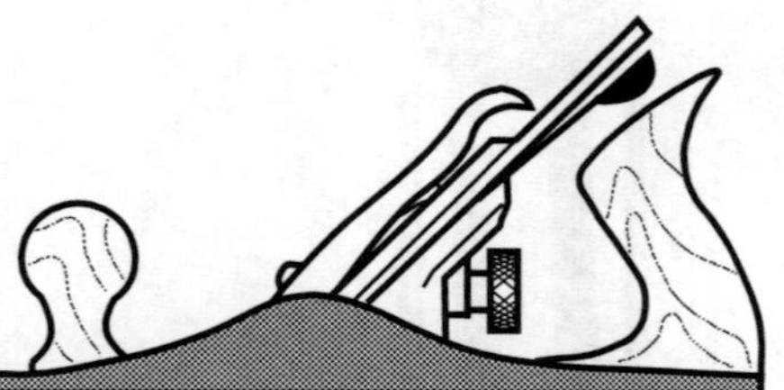

1 ____ 1 0

2 ____ 1 0

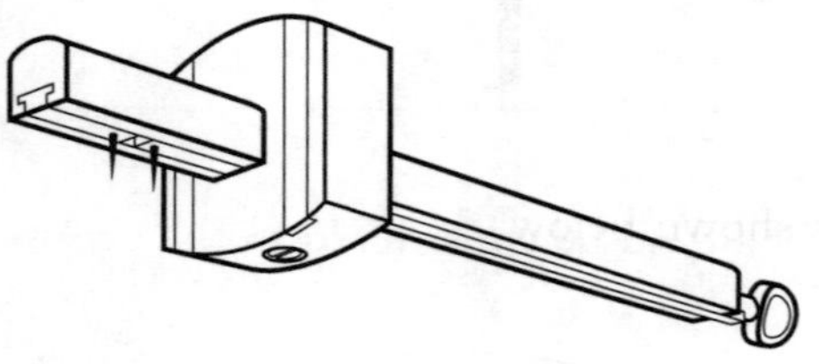

1 ____ 1 0

2 ____ 1 0

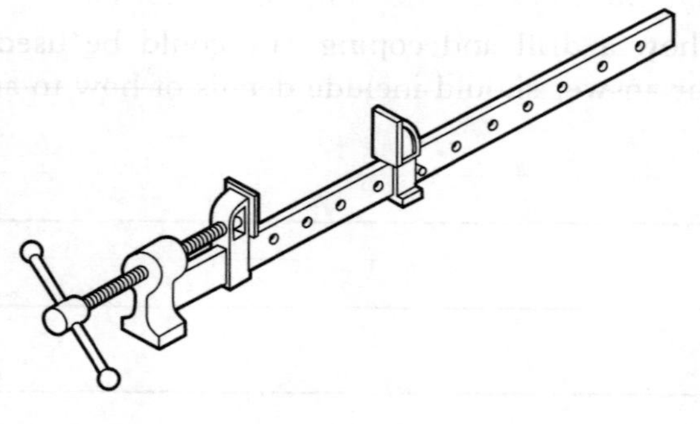

1 ____ 1 0

2 ____ 1 0

4. A table lamp is shown below.

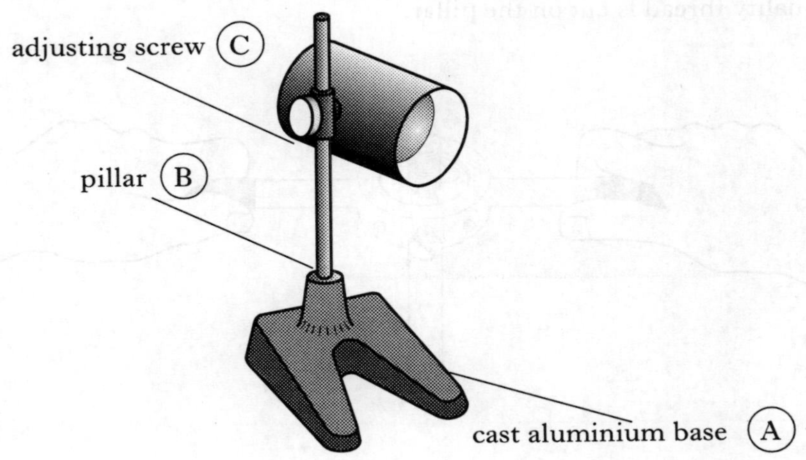

(*a*) State why aluminium is commonly used for casting in the school workshop.

____ **1 0**

(*b*) List **three** points which should be considered in the production of the pattern for the base.

(i) ____ **1 0**

(ii) ____ **1 0**

(iii) ____ **1 0**

(*c*) Write a short note on **each** of the following casting terms.

Cope and Drag ____

____

____ **1 0**

Runner and Riser ____

____

____ **1 0**

(*d*) The pillar is screwed into the aluminium base. State **one** procedure to ensure a high quality thread is cut on the pillar.

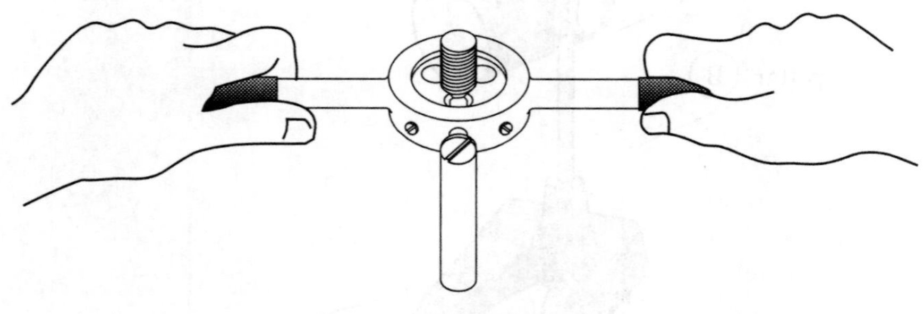

____ 1
____ 0

(*e*) State **one** reason for the textured surface found on the adjusting screw.

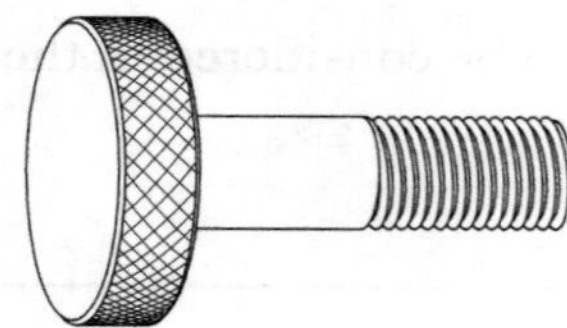

____ 1
____ 0

(*f*) State **three** general reasons why a change in lathe speed may be necessary when turning metal.

1 ____ 1 0

2 ____ 1 0

3 ____ 1 0

5. An incomplete analysis table is shown below. This table was produced by a pupil when asked to design a piece of jewellery.

A	B	C	D	E
Type	Theme	User Group		
Pendant	Ethnic	Boy		
Earring	Abstract	Girl		
Badge	Natural Form	Teenager		
Bangle	Football	Dad		
Hair Slide	Pop Music	Mum		
Brooch	Athletics	Gran		
	Cartoons	Student		

2 1 0

(*a*) (i) Insert suitable headings to columns D and E. **2 1 0**

(ii) Add at least three entries under each new heading.

(*b*) Choose a word from each column (A to E) in order to stimulate ideas for a piece of jewellery suitable for a boy interested in sport.

A ____________________

B ____________________

C ____________________

D ____________________ **2 1 0**

E ____________________

6. Two bicycles are shown.

1840

1990

Suggest **two** factors which may have influenced the development of bicycle design over the past 150 years.

1 ______________________________ 1 0

2 ______________________________ 1 0

7. The screwdriver shown was made from a single piece of high carbon steel. The handle was coated using a plastic powder.

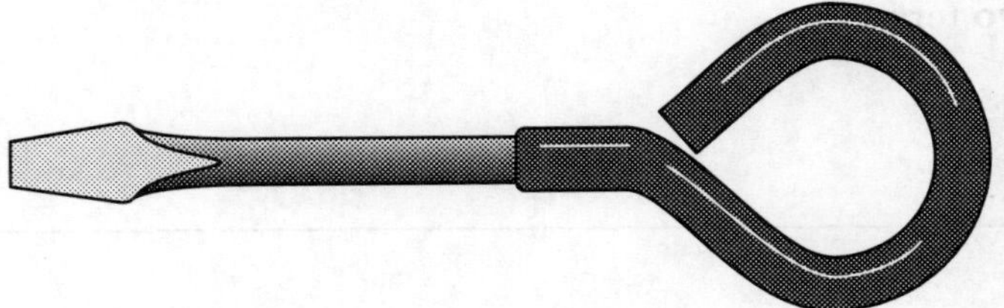

(*a*) Suggest **two** reasons for applying a plastic finish to the handle.

1 ____ 1 0

2 ____ 1 0

(*b*) Describe how you could produce identically shaped handles on a number of screwdrivers.

____

____

____ 1 0

(*c*) The tip of the screwdriver was hardened and tempered. Describe how this is carried out.

____

____

____

____

____

____

____ 3 2 1 0

(*d*) The screwdriver was designed with *function* in mind rather than *aesthetics*. Explain these **two** terms.

(i) Function

1 0

(ii) Aesthetics

1 0

(*e*) A clear thermoplastic sheet was formed to produce packaging to allow the screwdriver to be displayed in a DIY store.

(i) Name the process used to form the plastic packaging.

1 0

(ii) What is meant by the term thermoplastic?

1 0

(iii) Name a thermoplastic.

1 0

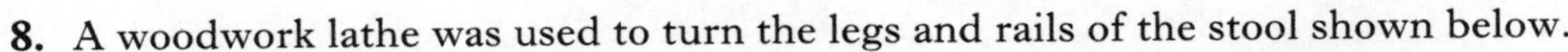

8. A woodwork lathe was used to turn the legs and rails of the stool shown below.

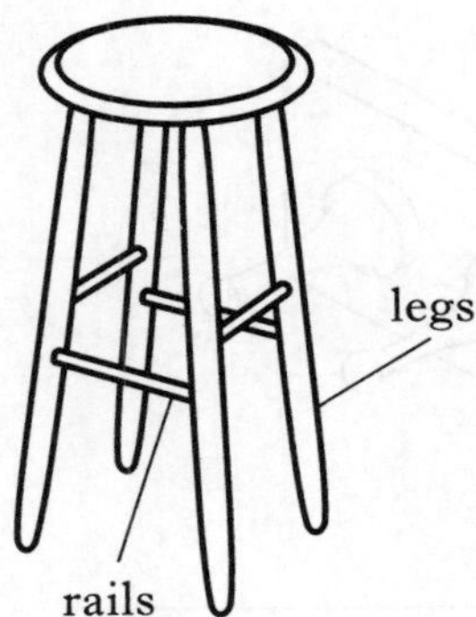

(*a*) The legs and rails are different lengths. Which part of the lathe needs to be moved to allow for the different lengths of legs and rails?

____

____ **1 0**

(*b*) Explain why the lathe, set up as shown, would not allow the best possible finish to be achieved when sanding.

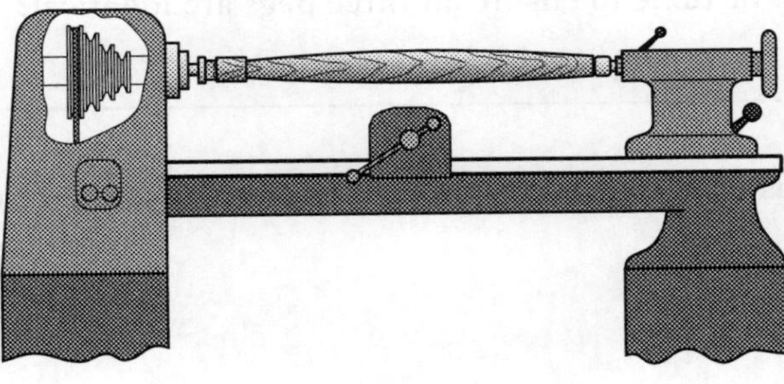

____

____

____ **1 0**

(*c*) Explain why the wood turning tools have long handles.

____

____

____ **1 0**

(*d*) A kitchen rack with three turned wooden pegs is shown below.

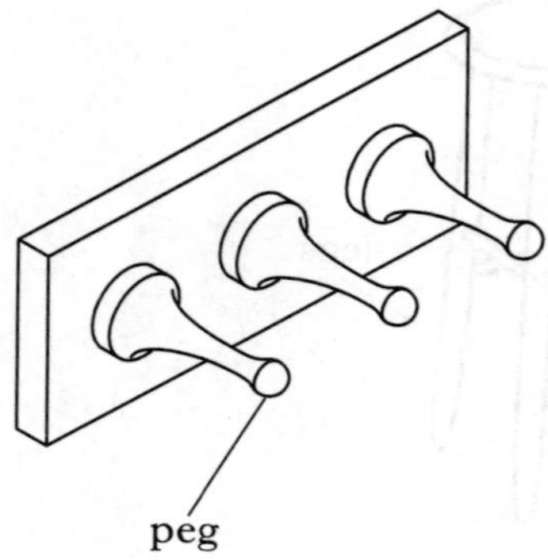

(i) Name a suitable European hardwood.

____ 1 0

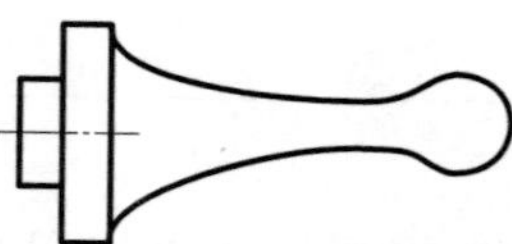

(ii) What could be done to ensure all three pegs are identical?

____ 1 0

(iii) A gouge was used to produce the curves on the pegs. Sketch the blade of this tool.

1 0

(iv) State **three** reasons for applying a finish to the rack.

1 ____ 1 0

2 ____ 1 0

3 ____ 1 0

9. The shower shown is designed to be used by people in the *5th* to the *95th percentile* range.

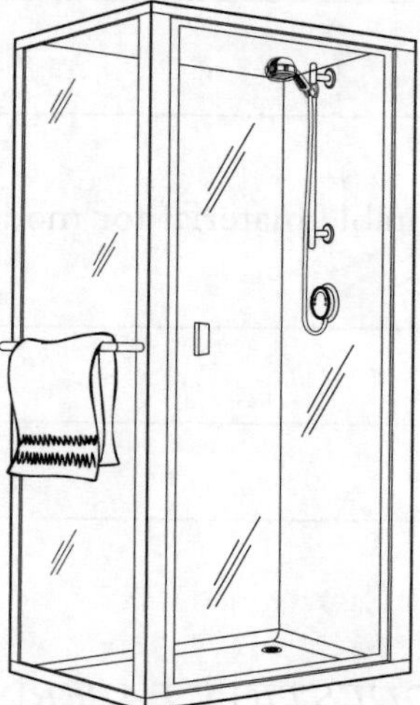

(*a*) State a **size** or **feature** of this design that takes into account:

(i) a 5th percentile consideration;

____ 1 0

(ii) a 95th percentile consideration.

____ 1 0

(*b*) Showers can be adjusted to make them accessible.
List **two** other products which are adjustable to suit human differences. In each case, state **one** adjustment.

	Product	**Adjustment**	
1	____________	____________	
		____________	1 0
2	____________	____________	
		____________	1 0

10. (*a*) State **two** reasons why modelling can be useful when designing.

1 ____ 1 0

2 ____ 1 0

(*b*) Why would plasticine be a suitable material for modelling a computer mouse?

____

____

____ 1 0

[*END OF QUESTION PAPER*]

Printed by Bell & Bain, Ltd., Glasgow, Scotland.

SOLUTIONS AND WORKED EXAMPLES

This series of books provides clear answers, simple explanations and sound advice for students PREPARING TO PASS a particular examination.
Most of the solutions are accompanied by a line-by-line commentary explaining the reasoning behind each step and some of the books have a chart showing the frequency with which the topics have appeared in the examination over a ten-year period.

Worked Examples Higher Maths ISBN 0 7169 3148 6 £4.30
The following books are designed to be used alongside the actual past paper books and contain fully worked solutions in a clear and simple manner to all questions.
Solutions to General Mathematics ISBN 0 7169 3238 5 £4.10
Solutions to Credit Mathematics ISBN 0 7169 3239 3 £4.10
Solutions to Higher Mathematics ISBN 0 7169 3240 7 £4.20
Solutions to Higher Physics ISBN 0 7169 3241 5 £4.20
Solutions to Higher Chemistry ISBN 0 7169 3242 3 £4.20

REVISION

Revise Your 'S' History ISBN 0 7169 3202 4 Covers the five most popular Contexts, namely Units 1B & C; 2B; 3C & D, and gives the basic facts required for candidates sitting the examination. Also includes worked examples to give the necessary examination technique on how to answer questions. £5.60
Revise Your Higher History Volume 1 ISBN 0 7169 6011 7 Fully covers Option C Sections (a) & (b) and Special Topic 11 and includes a list of useful titles for the extended essay. £4.80
Revise Your Higher History Volume 2 ISBN 0 7169 6013 3 Fully covers Option C Sections (a) & (c) and Special Topic 12 and includes a list of useful titles for the extended essay. £4.80
Revise Your Higher Mathematics ISBN 0 7169 6677 8 This book contains many worked examples of the types of questions candidates are likely to meet in the examination. Most of the solutions are accompanied by sound advice clarifying the mathematical procedures. £5.50

SELF TEST

Test Your 'C' Chemistry Calculations ISBN 0 7169 3169 9 Worked examples and graded questions covering the types of questions likely to be met at Credit Level. £3.30
Test Your 'C' Mathematics ISBN 0 7169 3209 1 For self-testing and revision of the Knowledge and Understanding aspect of the new Credit examination. With answers. £3.30
Test Your 'G' Mathematics ISBN 0 7169 3142 7 For self-testing and revision of the Knowledge and Understanding aspect of the new General examination. With answers. £3.30
Test Your Higher Mathematics ISBN 0 7169 3187 7 This book contains test questions, all answered, to give practice for candidates in sitting the Higher Mathematics examination. £3.30
Test Your Higher Chemistry ISBN 0 7169 3192 3 Fully covering the course, this book gives test questions in K&U and PS for self-testing and revision purposes. All questions answered and some with additional explanations. £5.30
Test Your Higher Chemistry Calculations ISBN 0 7169 3211 3 Covers all the types of question likely to be met in the examination. Includes worked examples and answers to questions. £6.50
Progressive Problems 'S' Grade Physics ISBN 0 7169 3233 4 Covers the topics studied for the syllabus and contains a planned sequence of questions from the simplest to the most difficult of problems. £6.50

SPECIMEN PAPERS

Credit Mathematics Specimen Papers ISBN 0 7169 8009 6 £3.10
General Mathematics Specimen Papers ISBN 0 7169 8010 x £3.10
These books each contain four model test papers to give you additional practice for the examination. With answers.
'S' Grade German Specimen Papers ISBN 0 7169 8002 9 Four sets of papers for 'F', 'G' and 'C' candidates covering Reading, Speaking and Writing. Answer guide for the Reading Papers. £4.40
'S' Grade Physics Specimen Papers ISBN 0 7169 8003 7 Six sets of model papers comprising three at General Level and three at Credit Level with all questions fully answered. £3.40
'H' Grade French Specimen Papers ISBN 0 7169 8012 6 £4.40
'H' Grade German Specimen Papers ISBN 0 7169 8439 3 Gives Reading, Essay and Cloze Test practice. Includes Reading Test answer scheme and Advice Section explaining each Paper. £4.40

MODULES

Worked Examples for Core 3 Mathematics ISBN 0 7169 3189 3 £4.40
Worked Examples for Core 4 Mathematics ISBN 0 7169 3190 7 £4.40
These books give practice exercises covering the first four of the five tests necessary for success.

Credit & General
CRAFT & DESIGN

ROBERT GIBSON · Publisher

17 Fitzroy Place, Glasgow, G3 7SF, Scotland, U.K.

Tel: 0141 248 5674 Fax: 0141 221 8219
e.mail: Robert .GibsonSons@btinternet.com
for availability and prices.

Prices are subject to alteration without notice.

ISBN 0 7169 9295 7